LOUISE TARRIER

The Way of the Sea Priestess

An inner path

Cover, and Illustrations by Gill Robinson
http://www.zhibit.org/gillrobinson

Matador
9 Priory Business Park
Kibworth Beauchamp
Leicestershire LE8 0RX, UK
Tel: (+44) 116 279 2299
Fax: (+44) 116 279 2277
Email: books@troubador.co.uk
Web: www.troubador.co.uk/matador

ISBN 978 1780882 505

British Library Cataloguing in Publication Data.
A catalogue record for this book is available from the British Library.

Typeset by Troubador Publishing Ltd, Leicester, UK

Matador is an imprint of Troubador Publishing Ltd

Printed and bound in the UK by TJ International, Padstow, Cornwall

To All Those Who Love & Care for the Oceans

Contents

1

Preface

This is an introduction to the esoteric ways of the Sea Priestess. I read Dion Fortune's book *The Sea Priestess* and was immediately drawn to this mythological title and to the elusive Morgan le Fay. I felt that I knew and understood this mysterious woman and I had a desire to share my knowledge with others. The book started me on a personal journey to remember and reclaim. *The Sea Priestess* was written in the 1930's when esoteric knowledge was truly 'hidden from view'. Dion Fortune approached this by giving knowledge in the form of a story. A tale of the magical workings of Vivien Morgan Le Fay and Wilfred a rather, sickly, strait laced and apathetic young man who is bullied and dismissed by the women in his life.

Morgan is a mystery throughout the book including her eventual disappearance. As the story unfolds she shows Wilfred the ways of magic and they journey together to discover their previous incarnations; Morgan as an ancient Atlantean Sea Priestess and Wilfred as the young man sacrificed to the Goddess of the Sea. With the help of the Priest of the Moon they journey into magical realms following the path of the moon and tides. After Morgan disappears Wilfred realises she is gone from his life forever but he finds new love with a young woman called Molly and also discovers that Morgan has left him a legacy in the form of her notes and journals.

In the book we are told that Molly reads these journals and learns the ways of the Sea Priestess, but we do not find out how she does this. We are left with the tantalising knowledge that all women can learn these secrets but we are unsure how. This book is an attempt to give the reader an insight into the journal that Morgan may have left behind. It also explores my own understanding of what a 'Sea Priestess' was and is, now and for the future.

In Fortune's book we are told that as Sea Priestesses Morgan and Molly sing to the sea. Their songs are different and yet they have a harmonic resonance with all of life, and are an embodiment of both the Goddess and the woman who sings.

'I am the Star that rises from the sea
The twilight sea.
I bring men dreams that rule their destiny.
I bring the dream-tides to the souls of men;
The tides that ebb and flow and ebb again
These are my secret, these belong to me
I am the eternal woman, I am She!
The tides of all men's souls belong to me.
The tides that ebb and flow and ebb again;
The silent, inward tides that govern men.
These are my secret, these belong to me.
Out of my hands he takes his destiny.
Touch of my hands confers polarity.
These are the moon-tides, these belong to me-
Hera in heaven, on Earth, Persephone;
Levanah of the tides, and Hecate.
Diana of the Moon, Star of the Sea
Isis unveiled and Ea, Binah, Ge!' (*The Sea Priestess,* Dion Fortune pg 167-168)

Within this book you will learn about the ways of the Sea Priestess as I have discovered them within my own practice, and in following the exercises you will find your own song and the song lines that stretch around the globe. I discovered my personal song through following this practice and it brings me many blessings.

Each individual will approach the book in their own way and its designed so that you can start the exercises at any point in the year. It's important that you read chapters two to six first and undertake the exercises within them; as this will give you the basic understanding and grounding you need to develop your relationship with the moon. Working through these chapters will also allow you to establish the link between your inner and outer world.

The way of the Sea Priestess is a feminine mystery and has been written with women primarily in mind. The tone is feminine and it is written as if speaking to a woman and I make no apologies for that. It is possible though for all of the exercises to be undertaken by men as well and the reclaiming of the Sea Priestess tradition is one that men can also champion.

The format of the book is set into seasons and the exercises within should be undertaken during that season and are not intended to be concurrent. I wrote the book for my own journey as a Sea Priestess and whilst some of the teachings within it will resonate, some may not. The book is intended as a guide and signpost and not to encompass all of the knowledge you will need and want. There are many resources available to a keen Sea Priestess and it is hoped you will begin the journey and then add your own experience. Keeping your moon diary and a journal where you document your own journey is highly recommended.

My sincerest wish is that through this book you develop a relationship with the Goddess within and without, and that you share this knowledge with other women. This book is dedicated to the wonderful Priestess and Goddess loving women and men in my life. Finally to my husband, my two sons and extended family who provide me with the ultimate magic of love.

Blessed be
Louise

2

An Inner Path

The way of the Sea Priestess is an inner path; it is a path of dreaming your world into creation. You become the container, the vessel, the feminine principal, the grail continuously opening your heart and allowing. Dion Fortune used the name 'Sea Priestess' in her 1930's novel of the same name. Vivien Morgan Le Fay sets about performing a natural work of magic and in the process she draws in Wilfred who, caught in the tidal flow of her work, sees and experiences the natural forces of magic within his own life. Like the Sea Priestess of Fortune's imaginings, we can positively influence the world and to call oneself a Sea Priestess is to have the deepest reverence for the natural world and to take full responsibility for your actions within it.

I believe that the mythological title of Sea Priestess recognises and re-energises an archetype that lives within the subconscious of many. For me it is a description of my core being and as I work with it there is a deep resonance within my subconscious. I believe that through identification and resonance with our archetypal selves that we truly allow our creative force to be at its most productive. We can recognise this when we are called in a very deep way to places or experiences. A call to the ocean or the waterways is a very strong calling for many, particularly for those who live in an island home such as the UK where I live and where the sea is an ever-near presence. In living and understanding our archetype we can integrate those parts of our psyche that we may have repressed and we can remember who we truly are.

The Priestess path that we follow as a Sea Priestess is an internal one, illuminating the inner self. It is a path of inner change and transformation. It is an allowing, for like water it follows the path of least resistance but then steadily changes the landscape of the psyche. Once you have been empowered by water you have to go with the flow. It is possible that while you journey the waters may become choppy and you can feel overwhelmed. Therefore it is not a path that should be undertaken lightly and it is important that those who wish to follow the way of the Sea Priestess put in place a support network for those times when the flow is blocked or feels as if it is flowing out of control.

The greatest magic is the transformation of the self, and it is our imagining of this self that we undertake in the practice; the world is a reflection of our thoughts and the Sea Priestess works towards ensuring that those thoughts are the journey she wishes to undertake in this lifetime. It is a great truth that the only change we can truly undertake is the change of the self; through this path we can initiate change in our environment, within our relationships and in all with whom we come into contact; as it is our perspective that shifts, so that we become all that we can be. The Sea Priestess works with the forces of nature, earth, air, fire and water to transform her and in doing so transforms all of her life circumstances.

In this practice we experience the Goddesses of water, for

we are working with the feminine principle; we are the vessel for our thoughts, feelings, mind, body and spirit. We experience the feminine as receiver, holder of wisdom and we find the Goddess within our own compassion and innate inner wisdom. The practice is one of transformation and we align ourselves with the healing powers of water to transform, cleanse, nurture and bring forth life.

In ancient times the crossing of water took the ancients to the other world; the place of spirit, we will travel to these places to reclaim our soul selves. We will utilise the metaphor of the Grail as the womb space and the source of all creation. Working closely with the cycles of the moon and the tides and the gravitational pull she exerts upon our bodies as well as the Earth. We will enter the dreamtime and work with the inner worlds and the spaces between that hold the potential of new creation. As we work with the natural cycles and rhythms of our bodies, then we can allow for the natural resting and energetic periods we experience and we will find that we become more productive, more creative and ultimately more in tune with all that surrounds us.

This book is a journey into the ways of the Sea Priestess; for those who follow the exercises they will be opening their world to the natural forces of life. It is a steady unfolding of experience through surrender and the letting go of the desire to control that in its self is illusionary. We open our hearts to receive the wisdom of the Goddess, allowing Her to guide us and show us our true natures. We become the vessel for Her allowing ourselves to be filled, our hearts opening ever wider to her love.

To call oneself a Priestess is to invoke an archetype that in today's world is little understood. By naming ourselves in this way we are often inviting the ridicule, amusement or misunderstanding of others. We need to understand what the term 'Priestess' means to us as individuals and the image we would wish to reflect to others. We're the actors in this scene and when others see us as Priestess through our actions, words and deeds we become that which we seek. For it is our definition of Priestess that is important rather than the views of others. There are a number of definitions available but instead of seeking the answer externally it is 'I feel' more appropriate to look within. What does this archetype mean to us as individuals? When we meditate or travel to the inner worlds, what impression do we have of our Priestess selves? We would do well to retain the fluidity of water and to allow our definition to grow and shape itself over time, rather than narrowly confining it to another's approximation.

For me the journey is never ending and when I first called myself Priestess I had little understanding of what that would mean in my life or where my journey would take me. What I have found is that this still remains true for I have found the image shape shifting as my own journey deepens. What we need to remember is that in our projection of ourselves as Priestess, we are adding to this archetypal energy and we should do so with reverence and respect to those who have walked the path before and will walk the path after us.

In awakening an archetype such as the Sea Priestess we are claiming an ancient tradition that resonates in the sub-conscious world and when we bring it forth we are breathing new life and energy into it and calling forth something from our deepest soul memory. We are creating anew, for in this time the Sea Priestess only exists through our actions and our deeds. We should seek to do her justice.

We are surrendering to the Goddess. We are offering her our lives, relinquishing control and trusting and knowing that she will guide us to a place of inner and outer fulfillment. In surrendering to her she will take us to that place of joy, for her love will fuel our passions and enable us to create the life we truly wish to live. We will follow our hearts desire. Yet to get to that place of surrender is a journey that can be as easy or as difficult as we choose to make it. The illusion that we have control in our lives is just that, an illusion. While planning for the future, worrying about what may or may not happen and whether we can control its path, we are not living our lives for we are missing the present and that is all that truly exists.

We can choose to fill each moment in the way we would like to live it and in doing so the future becomes irrelevant for we are building it moment by moment, each moment fully savoured and lived to its fullest. So therefore there can never be regret for the past. To live this way in our modern society is difficult for we are bombarded with images of how we should be, what we should buy and how we should live. We learn through the experience of our culture that if we only had 'x' then we will truly be happy. We are told by society that we need to take care of our futures but we are rarely told that the best way to do this is to act truly in the present. We are encouraged to burden our lives with material things, to become indebted and to strive for a better life that always exists tomorrow. When tomorrow or the things arrive then the cycle begins again and we remain unsatisfied, unfulfilled and unhappy. Breaking this cycle can be extremely difficult because by doing so we are breaking the norms of our society. Yet we can begin in small ways, in the now, by positively living in the present. Doing the things we need to do today and not procrastinating and putting things off. We can jump in with both feet and live the day. We can try and break the habit of worrying about tomorrow by allowing our thoughts but not heeding them. In doing so we assess whether we can do anything now in this moment to alleviate the worry and then doing it; and if not, recognising that we can do nothing today and therefore we have done all that we can do and letting the thought go.

In deepening our journey we open ourselves to our emotional body, to our expressive state, we record how we feel and allow our emotions rather than repressing or denying them. This requires great courage. Often the word emotional is used to imply weakness or lack of rational thought. Recently though, the idea of 'emotional intelligence' has been a metaphor for describing people who have an inbuilt intuitive self-knowledge which aids in their interactions and communication with others. In expressing our emotions we are allowing our bodies to be emotionally intelligent and providing a pathway toward internal fulfillment. In following this path you enable your emotions to have adequate and releasing expression. Whether it is through artistic, verbal or inner healing work. This takes courage, as it requires surrender and the letting go of expectation to truly work with Goddess in divine partnership.

As you follow the way of the Sea Priestess you will walk the spiral of the Goddess as she represents herself in the seasonal wheel of the year. You will learn through experiencing her energies as you journey with her. You will experience her energies in the new, waxing, full and waning moons, moving in the ebb and flow of the energies that present; attuning your body and your mind to her rhythms. In this way you will learn how to truly know this path and know yourself.

Energy of Water

The way of the Sea Priestess utilises the metaphors of water and of the moon, the ebb and the flow of our lives from maiden, through lover, mother and crone, the waxing and waning of our energies as we pursue different paths. In ancient times the mother Goddess was the water of life, she was the fish Goddess representing the new life that emerges from the sea.

Water is one of the fundamentals of life and it is no surprise that the earliest civilizations were founded next to oceans, rivers and natural waterways. Water, as well as providing us with one of life's basic needs, also supplies us with food from the many creatures that live within it. Some of the earliest Goddesses known to us are associated with water and its life giving properties. Our ancestors were dependent upon the seasonal harvest and rains (as we are today, even though we may feel more remote from the process) and Mother Earth was petitioned for the seasonal rains. Our link to water and its connection to the divine and sacred is something that stretches back into the very mists of time for this *'blue planet'* our home; is a watery planet and it is from water that we owe our very existence.

'They conceived all beings as coming forth from the sea, and

they were right, for there was a time when the waves covered the Earth…then came the time when they learnt the part of the father, and they looked in nature for the fecundating father of all and perceived it to be the sun. So they adored the sun as well as the sea; but the cult of the sea is older, for she is the Great Mother.' (The Sea Priestess, Dion Fortune pg 127*)*

I believe that water is a living consciousness that has been with us since the beginning of time. It flows through us connecting us to it and each other. Within many spiritual paths there is a concept that we are not separate from the divine but that we all carry it within us; that when we meet with another our spiritual selves recognise this as truth; truth that we are all connected and that it is only our ego selves that separate us from this divine connection. If water is conceived of as a living spiritual consciousness then there can be no better metaphor for spirit, as it is the most palpable physical aspect that we can utilise flowing through us and connecting us to each other and to the planet. The ancients and tribal peoples of the world understood this relationship and water, and the connections that we can make when we work with this spiritual presence can be life changing and profound. The Sea Priestess works at understanding this connection and bringing it into her life on a daily basis. To achieve this we work with Goddesses that represent different qualities of water and of our essential selves bringing the two together in magical alchemy.

As you work with the different Goddesses at each of the seasonal points of the year, you celebrate their aspects as well as water in its many forms and you learn the nature and associations of each Goddess so that you can integrate them into your daily life.

You work at devising your own song. The song of the Sea Priestess that is sung to the waters, bringing healing to your life and that of the water, this is your own individual song and a method of communicating with the water and the consciousness that is the water. Like the whales and the dolphins you add your song to the memories held within it.

You also work with the moon in all its aspects, for it is through the moon that we see the reflection of ourselves and the mirror of our inner journey in the outer world. In Dion Fortune's book it is the Goddess Isis who is at the centre of her work and you will work with the veiled Goddess calling her as the All Mother in this practice.

The All Mother

The Egyptians worshiped Isis and she is an ancient divinity but the story is much older than the Egyptian civilization. She was originally Ge, the ancient mother who is Goddess of this planet who was the Paleolithic mother Goddess worshipped by our ancestors for millennia. She was the fish, the bird, the bear, the bee and the serpent Goddess. From her body all were born and then returned to her to be reborn anew. She was the womb of the Earth, and our own cycles were mirrored in her nature, and all of her nature was sacred.

The ancient Formoire of the Gaelic tales called this Goddess of the ancestors from whom we all came and who birthed us from her waters, Domnu. She is lady of the Oceans; Queen of the deep, from Her waters all life emerges. She is the water's of life, the waters of the womb, the embryonic fluid from which we all emerge as we begin our lives. The Goddess Domnu represents our compassion; she is the flowing of our emotions and the strength and wisdom of water. She is water as the feminine principal represented by the Chalice, the Grail. She is the vessel that holds all of creation, the womb from which all life is born. She is the Chalice, the womb space that we will use to harness our creative spirit and to transform our lives.

Domnu is the great water mother. Her creatures are the creatures of the seas and the oceans. The giant whales whose song are the symphonies of the seas, the playful intelligent dolphins, the selkies and the seals, all of the mammals that live in her waters, bearing their young and reminding us of our ancient ancestry. She is the fish; the salmon of wisdom, the electrified creatures of the deep, the corals and the vegetation; she is all life that dwells within her waters, including you.

Domnu is the mermaid Goddess who is half woman, half fish; her bare breasted top half representing the mother of all, love, nourishment and nurture. She is life giver and yet her bottom half is fish: cold blooded, primeval, a mystery. She returns us to the sea to our death and eventual rebirth. She is the Undine, the water nymph and the siren that calls men to her depths; all of these mystical races are her creatures.

This ancient mother became Isis of the Egyptians with her own story. She was the Goddess of the Nile peoples who depended on the rivers flooding, its ebb and flow to provide them with their crops and livelihoods. She was Queen of the heavens of the Earth and of the underworld.

The flooding of the Nile valley was a representation of the

Goddess on the land for from its ebb and flow, new life was created. As the waters evaporated the land became dust but then magically the floodwater would come and the land would be renewed, life would teem back into the valley. Isis the Goddess is protector, mother, lover and wife, with the ultimate power of death, life and rebirth. Isis is the representation of the Nile, her story that of bringing life back to life the dying Osiris, gathering the parts of his body together and breathing new life into them so that she may conceive Horus, their child. Osiris is her brother/husband, she conceives his son Horus and then nurtures the child when Osiris passes to the underworld. Isis constantly has to search for Osiris and then awaken him. Through finding him she brings the Earth back to life and together they represent the cycle of the flooding Nile and the moon. Isis is central to this lunar mystery a cyclical movement of dark into light.

It is with the All Mother, Ge, Domnu, and Isis in all her guises, and all her names that you will work with in this practice calling her presence into the space in which you work, tuning into her energies so that she is present in all her faces as the seasons turn.

I have been fortunate in my life to be able to train as a Priestess of Avalon with Kathy Jones in Glastonbury/Avalon. A magical experience brought to life by this wonderful woman who has spent her life in service to the Goddess. Working with other Priestesses and immersing myself in Goddess teachings, I am called to expand the goal of mystical immersion and unification and to work with the Goddesses of water.

All my life I have lived close to the sea around Britain and for a while the Indian Ocean. I have walked the beaches, swam in the waters, listened to the tide and the rising and falling of the beach, the noise sending me into a deep sleep. I have felt her majesty as stormy weather, the power and intensity of her seas. I have witnessed the destruction that can arise as roads and homes are swept away and boats wrecked by the immensity of the power of water. Sadly we have all witnessed the devastation and destruction that water can create, and even if we only saw from our TV screens, we have all been affected by the two massive tsunamis that hit the Indian Ocean and the Japanese coast in recent years.

These tsunamis have been a stark reminder of the power of the oceans. My deepest feelings when near water, though, have always been my gratitude for all that I have and am as I have stood looking out to the faraway horizon.

I personally feel called to work with the Goddess energies in this manifestation and to know her as she truly is: a beautiful, bountiful, dark and azure fully formed Goddess of creation and of death and rebirth. As you journey the wheel of the year, you will place the All Mother at the centre of your life as well and you will find the things that represent her in your life and in your relationship with her.

3

An Introduction to the Practice

The Sea Priestess Practice

This book is designed as a series of exercises that you follow throughout the year. You can start the exercises at any point of the year, and each of the chapters can be followed in isolation. In this chapter you will learn about the wheel of the year (or the medicine wheel as it's also known) and about the Goddesses I associate with that time of the year and the seasonal blessings they bring.

You will discover how the practice can be integrated into your daily life and you will learn about the energy system within your body, known as the 'chakras'. You will also learn a simple grounding exercise. It is important that you work through this chapter first as it provides some basic knowledge that will be used throughout the whole book.

Goddesses of the Wheel

The exercises in the seasonal chapters allow you to attune yourself with the energies and Goddesses of that particular season. The seasons are split into Winter, (Samhain and Yule), Spring, (Imbolc and Spring Equinox), Summer, (Beltane and Summer Solstice) and finally Autumn, (Lammas and Autumn Equinox). The seasonal focus is based on the eight pagan festivals of the year. At each point in the year different Goddesses are presented within the practice and they have an association with each season. This is called a 'wheel of the year' or a 'medicine wheel'.

The wheel is circular and split into four sections each representing a seasonal point. There is also a central hub that represents the inner self and this is where the Goddess as All Mother is placed. The wheel is representative of life demonstrating the passing of the seasons, and our journey through life. Each season has a Goddess with a connection with water and with whom I have experienced a personal connection. Each season is also associated with a moon phase. When working with a medicine wheel you move around the wheel changing your start point as the seasons change:

Samhain	31st October
Yule	21st December
Imbolc	2nd February
Oestre/Spring Equinox	21st March
Beltane	1st May
Summer Solstice	21st June
Lammas	1st August
Mabon/Autumn Equinox	21st September

In the southern hemisphere you will need to turn the wheel around, so for example, Beltane 1st May would become Samhain 31st October.

As you move through the year you learn about the Goddess in all her different aspects and the stages of a woman's life. 'As above, so below.' This allows your inner practice to resonate with the energies of the outer world and you align yourself with what is happening in nature and the seasons.

At the centre of the wheel is the Goddess as All Mother. She represents all aspects of the Goddess. The Goddesses I have chosen for the wheel are deliberately representative of many cultures, paths and traditions but you can chose to follow your own wheel based on local Goddesses, or change the place of the Goddess on the wheel if intuitively it feels more right. There is no right or wrong way but instead the wheel acts as a signpost leading you to research and find anew the Goddesses who have meaning for you.

The Goddesses of the Wheel

At Samhain, the old Celtic New Year where the veil between the inner and outer world is thin, we meet with Vivienne, Lady of the Lake, the Goddess who gave Arthur his sword and the right to rule Britain. She is the bestower of Kingship, the ancient Goddess who gave men the right to rule if they worked on her behalf and that of the land. She is death and re-birth and it is Vivienne who takes the souls of the dead to their afterlife or restoration across the lake. In the Glastonbury myth, the island is Avalon, the isle of Apples; Inys Witrin, the glass isle. Vivienne speaks to us in dreams and in myth and we lie still in the dark, waiting for our rebirth into the springtime, into the star fire. She is the source of all wisdom and we can journey with her as Priestess Shaman to the underworld. The cauldron from which she nourishes us through our journey in the afterlife represents her waters.

As the wheel turns towards Yule we find Sedna the Inuit Goddess, she is the protectress of the oceans and the creatures who dwell there. She is the bountiful grandmother and she is also the tumultuous and destructive nature of water that removes all from its path, so that the new can come forth. She is the dark and angry sea that takes men to its depths. She is the bounty of the ocean that feeds the lands, the primordial mother from which we all originated. She is abundance and destruction. We celebrate her as we move into the depths of winter and experience the ice and snow, and the stillness and silence this brings. Sedna is the Northern Goddess of the arctic circle peoples, whose livelihoods depend on the ocean and who travel into her deep waters at all times of the year. We pray to her for all the fishermen of the world who require safe passage.

At Imbolc we place Coventina, the Northern British Goddess of the springs and wells. Coventina is also associated with Minerva the Roman Goddess. The people of the past recognised the openings of the earth, such as springs and wells as openings into the mother Goddess herself. They were places of connection. They drank her clear waters and received her blessing and her healing. We can still experience this today and there are many springs and wells dedicated to Goddesses Worldwide. In Glastonbury (England) there are the red and white springs on the foothill of the Tor, which are still places of reverence where we can partake of the healing waters of the Goddess. At Imbolc we celebrate the Goddess as maiden and as the initiator. At the first stirrings of spring we make our wishes at her wells leaving our tribute of coins or offerings.

As Spring Equinox arrives we experience the Goddess as Sabrina, she holds the knowledge and wisdom of life, holding all at balance. Her rivers are the arteries of life running across the land, providing fresh water to sustain our lives. It is no surprise that most major cities are built alongside rivers as we dwell near the source. Sabrina is the spawning fish, the eggs that signify the start of new life and of birth. Her waters flood the land bringing about the greening and the new life that emerges. Sabrina is the Goddess of the River Severn with its unusual tidal surge.

At Beltane, directly opposite Samhain on the medicine wheel, we encounter Aphrodite. She is beauty and love and the Goddess of the fountain and the waterfall. Her waters are the emanations of the vulva. She is the Goddess who is enchantress and who offers the comfort of the thighs, she is the embodiment of desire, lust and love. She is the mirror in which we can find the beauty that resides within. This Greek Goddess teaches us the many qualities of love and the sensual nature of life.

At solstice where the sun reaches its zenith and the days are long and nights short, we discover Sulis, Goddess of the springs. She is best known as Sulis Minerva and the hot springs in Bath, England, represent her worship by the Romans who went to her bath houses to immerse themselves in the pleasure of her waters. Temples to her are found all over the south of England. Here the Goddess is pleasure, the enjoyment of the long summer days. Her warm waters take away all of the stresses and strains of our lives.

At Lammas we adventure with Boann, the Irish Goddess who gave her name to the river Boyne. She is a Goddess of the Tuatha De Danann and is found in the myths of the ancient Gaelic peoples. She is a water Goddess of sacrifice and mirrors the grain Goddess of the Earth. Boann brings forth the life giving waters of the river Boyne and yet at the same time loses her own life. She mirrors for us the ultimate sacrifice of the life giving mother.

As we move into autumn and the equinox, Yemanya the African Goddess of the oceans moves to centre stage. Her worship has travelled from Africa to Brazil where she is worshipped by the people who take to the beaches dressed in white and make offerings of flowers and small candles into the waters in her honour She is a mother Goddess and is often depicted as a mermaid. Her gifts are endless like the tide as one disappears another appears. She is fruition and she bestows all that we need upon us. She is the ever-giving mother who has only love and universal abundance to offer us as long as we ask.

At the centre of the wheel we find the great mother Goddess who is the All Mother and all aspects of the Goddess and us. She has many names and faces.

On the next page is a pictorial representation of the wheel of the year and the Goddesses of the season.

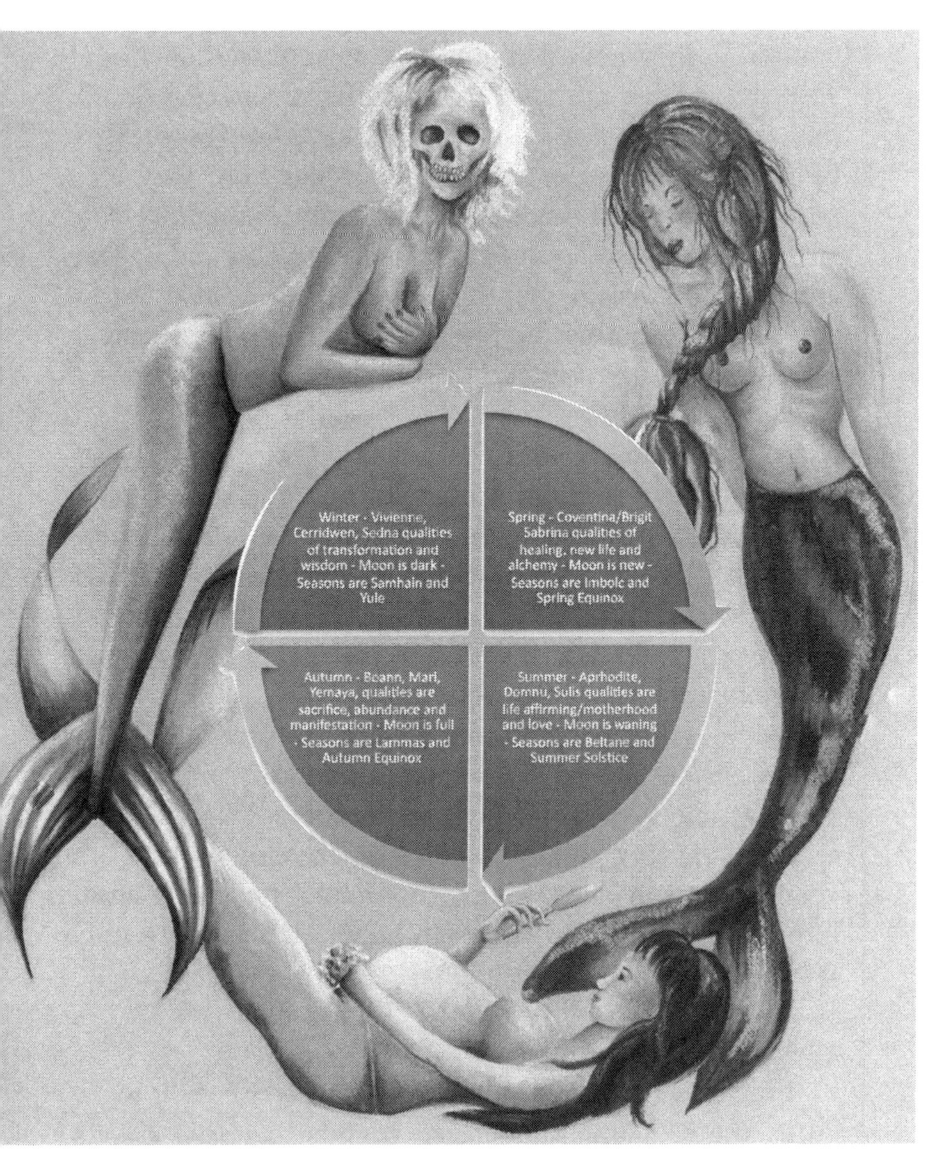
Winter - Vivienne, Cerridwen, Sedna qualities of transformation and wisdom - Moon is dark - Seasons are Samhain and Yule
Spring - Coventina/Brigit Sabrina qualities of healing. new life and alchemy - Moon is new - Seasons are Imbolc and Spring Equinox
Autumn - Boann, Mari, Yemaya, qualities are sacrifice, abundance and manifestation - Moon is full - Seasons are Lammas and Autumn Equinox
Summer - Aprhodite, Domnu, Sulis qualities are life affirming/motherhood and love - Moon is waning - Seasons are Beltane and Summer Solstice

Integrating The Practice Into Your life

The Sea Priestess practice is a spiritual one and in any spiritual practice you need to ensure that you anchor yourself to the physical as you develop your spiritual body. You are moving through many different energies; both physical and subtle and it is easy to find yourself adrift. This can manifest in not coping with your daily life, your job, and the chores and requirements of home and family. You are undertaking this journey to enhance your life and staying grounded will ensure that this is the case. As a Sea Priestess you are not escaping the physical world, you are working with it to enhance your experience and perception of it.

As you are working with the self this also includes your body and the water that flows within it. You should treat your body with respect and give it the diet and exercise program that enhances rather than diminishes your life force. For the purposes of following the book you should modify your diet where necessary to ensure that you are respecting the wisdom of your body.

However you should not change or modify any diet or medication prescribed by your doctor, and before undertaking any change in diet or exercise routine, it's wise to consult your doctor for their recommendation. The following five points are a guide to benefiting fully from this practice.

1. **Move**
   Every day try and get some form of exercise. Follow the example of our four legged friends and take a walk twice a day. A half hour yoga routine will also be very beneficial.

2. **Drink plenty of water**
   Where possible try to drink at least 2 litres of water every day. Avoid tap water that may have been contaminated with chemicals.

3. **Get enough sleep**
   Everybody's need for sleep varies but cortisol levels that regulate the metabolism can be disrupted if we aren't getting enough sleep. This can result in an inability to metabolise complex carbohydrates, which can cause blockages within the physical body and also cause unnecessary weight gain.

4. **Cut out alcohol and other stimulants such as caffeine**
   Artificial stimulants disrupt our body's natural rhythm and should therefore be avoided.

5. **Enjoy what you eat**
   Take time to prepare and eat your food. Enjoy it and bless the nourishment your body is receiving. Give thanks to the Goddess for the bounty of this planet that gives you all that you need.

The Sea Priestess works with all of nature, not just water, and attunes herself with the seasons and the forces of nature. The forces of nature are known as the 'Tattvas' or elements. There are four primary elements: earth, air, fire, and water; then there is the fifth element that is ether or spirit. By attuning yourself with these primary energies you are able to bring yourself into harmony with both the Earth and your own body, as we are all comprised of all the elements, as is the Earth and all the creatures upon it.

Chakras

Your body also has energy centres known as 'chakras' and when these are out of balance then this can manifest as illness or emotional distance. The chakras are representative of the elements that exist within nature inside your own body (see the chakra illustration).

At the base of our spine, located between the anus and the sex organs, is the first chakra that is also known as the 'base or root chakra'. This chakra is representative of earth energy; it is grounding and is responsible for your response to basic needs such as feeling stable and secure. This is the root of your internal energy system and is associated with the lower frequencies of light. Its colour is red. When this chakra is out of balance it can manifest as not feeling grounded, lacking energy and generally not feeling supported in life. Physically it can manifest as circulatory problems and a tendency towards cold hands and feet. At its most extreme the individual can suffer from exhaustion.

The second chakra is known as the 'sacral chakra' and it is located below the navel but above the pubic bone. Its colour frequency is orange and it is associated with the sexual response and creativity. It is traditionally associated with water and it is the womb chakra where our creativity is held, formed and given life. It is associated with the moon and dreaming and is therefore a very important chakra to activate when undertaking this journey. When out of balance it can manifest as a lack of flow to life and a lack of creative energy. Physically it can lead to loss of libido and rigidity of movement within the joints.

The third chakra is the 'solar plexus'; this is where we get our energy and life force. Its colour is yellow and this chakra is associated with fire energy. When unbalanced it can result in fear of life or unnecessary and irrational anger. Physically it can manifest as poor digestion and lack of absorption of nutrients into the body.

The fourth chakra is the 'heart chakra' and is associated with balance. Its colour is green and element air. This is the place that regulates our interactions with others. When our heart chakra is out of balance it can manifest as a lack of love both for yourself and others. It is where your compassion lives. Physically it can manifest as heart and lung problems and lack of oxygenation of the blood stream. When out of balance we can shut ourselves off from the world around us.

The first four chakras are about the body and the relationship between you and the outside world and the elements. There are three further chakras that are the throat, third eye and crown chakra. Their colours are blue, violet and white. They are our connection to spiritual truth. The throat chakra is blue and is about finding our inner truth. The chakra regulates our ability to find peace and is associated with the nervous system. This chakra can be activated by free expression. Singing, chanting and repeating mantras are ways of balancing this chakra.

The sixth chakra or 'third eye' is as its name suggests, located on the brow point between the eyes and is the chakra of intuition. When this chakra is blocked our natural intuitive natures are also blocked and our worldview can become skewed. Finally the 'crown chakra' is the seventh chakra and is our connection to spirit. Blockage in this chakra can cause confusion in our thought processes and we can feel disconnected both from the divine and ourselves.

Ensuring that your chakras remain balanced and that your body is in harmony is an essential part of this journey. Lack of balance in any area or over activation of any area may cause you to feel unwell, and you will certainly feel unbalanced and ungrounded within the practice if this happens. If you can at least once a week, try to get outside on the land, walking by the sea or in your local park or woodland. Being in nature helps to balance your chakras and keeps you in tune with the world around you. Other chakra or body balancing techniques, which are widely accessible, are yoga, reflexology and acupuncture. There are of course many others you can try and within this book there are also various exercises and practices that will ensure you remain balanced. One of the most essential body balancing techniques is to remain grounded. You can perform the grounding exercise illustrated below as often as you like and its benefits are enhanced when performed outdoors. So wrap up if necessary, make yourself get outside and you will find that this exercise and many of the others within the book take on a whole new dimension.

You should perform the grounding exercise below on a regular basis throughout the practice to ensure that you remain grounded and rooted in your life.

Grounding and Base Chakra Exercise

Stand with your feet evenly spaced about a foot apart and put your hands on your hips. Take five deep breaths, make sure that you fill your lungs as much as you can, you can breathe through the nose or the mouth whichever feels more comfortable. On the exhale, make sure that you exhale through your mouth making an audible sound as you do so. This breath is deeply relaxing and eliminating.

After the deep breaths, close your eyes and breathe normally but deeply. Listen to your breath as you inhale and exhale, (if you begin to feel dizzy or disorientated open your eyes for a moment) imagine the breath circulating throughout your body. Feel the oxygen reaching all the parts of your body, moving through your circulatory system re-energising it on the in breath and detoxifying it on the out breath. After a few minutes of just breathing, imagine your life force energy circulating around your body, moving down through your root chakra (the base of your spine), down through your feet into the ground below you. See that energy making its way down through the land, through the earth, through the rock and stone and the sub layers of earth, down deep into the Earth's core. Here your energy meets with the energies of the Earth Mother, feel her nurturing, loving energy mixing with your own. Feel your feet firmly rooted and planted into the ground like the roots of a tree. Draw the energy of mother Earth up through those roots into your body and feel her energy mixing with your life force; circulating around your body. You are totally connected with the Earth, as you breathe, you breathe with the pulse of the Earth itself. Stay like this for a while, breathing with the Mother Earth. When you are ready, release that energy and all of those things you wish to release into the Earth, allowing the mother to take them and turn them into energetic compost. Thank her for this time for this moment of grounding and release. Then open your eyes and repeat the five detoxifying breaths that you took at the start of the exercise.

Now read and perform the exercises in chapters four, five and six before beginning the practice

Notes

Notes

4

Priestesses of the Waters of Life

I believe that there was once an ancient sisterhood of women who called themselves Sea Priestesses; there was not one Sea Priestess but many. It was their role to commune with nature as it revealed itself through the waters on this blue planet. It was their divine purpose to communicate with the water as a life force. They ensured that the seas, rivers and oceans were cared for and that the true life giving nature of the Goddess was recognised and revered by all. They understood the mystery of water, that it was a sacred force that connected all of life. Through this shared connection they were able to communicate with all of her creatures. They worked with water to understand the wisdom of life itself. These ancient Sea Priestesses worked as groups of nine women and, like the other sisterhoods of mythology, they understood the qualities that resided within themselves and their sisterhood.

In Dion Fortune's *The Sea Priestess*, a glimpse of the past is seen as Morgan and Wilfred remember the ancient Sea Priestess who has come to save the land from being swallowed by the ocean.

'The Sea Priestess was a kind of Pythoness, and the gods spoke through her. Being a Pythoness, she was negative, passive, she did not make magic herself, but was an instrument of the priests.' (*The Sea Priestess,* Dion Fortune pg 108)

This 'I believe' is Fortune illustrating a distortion of the true nature of the ancient Sea Priestess, who was a seer and able to communicate with water as a living consciousness. She was not passive in order to do the work of priests, rather she was the communication channel between the natural world and human beings. Her magic was the ability to understand totally the forces of nature and to become at one with them. She communicated the power of the oceans in all their destructive and life giving forces. She didn't distinguish between good or bad, flood or drought; she remained passive and allowing, working with her fellow Sea Priestesses to communicate when the floods and droughts would come so that crops could be cultivated; and she warned people of natural disasters, such as Tsunami and flooding. Her job was to ensure that the water remained pure and full of positive intention so that the life force of all benefited. She was the guardian of the memory contained within the water. She knew that it was the spiritual connection of water that binds all of us to each other and to the planet. She was the link between Gaia and her people.

The Sea Priestesses also divined the future for they were in tune with all that was, is and will be. They were able to heal through the power of water by purifying it and they were able to cure illness and cleanse individuals of the diseases from which they suffered, whether these were physical or spiritual. This cellular healing was able to clear away existing karma and allow for the ascension of individuals to the knowledge of their true spiritual selves. This was in the first age of Atlantis before the distortions as illustrated in *The Sea Priestess* by Fortune, where the priests used the Sea Priestesses for their own ends, sacrificing the lives of men in order to influence the sea.

Of course nature runs its own course as water teaches us and this path was doomed to failure; the true nature of the Sea Priestess was lost, remaining only as a fragment of memory along with the Atlanteans themselves.

The original Atlantean Sea Priestesses used the constellation of the Pleiades and the moon to aid in their communication with the planet and the waters that flowed upon it. They worked in sisterhoods of nine mirroring the stars, as above so below. Dolphins and whales still carry the memory of these ancient times and the Sea Priestesses of old could channel their healing power in a similar way in which dolphins do now. These ancient memories of the Sea Priestesses are also still contained within the ice cores deep within Antarctica, where ancient Atlantis once was. As we move through the 21st Century it is time for these ancient memories to be unlocked once more and for the Sea Priestesses to return. The sentient being, which is the water of this planet, wishes to work with us; to impart wisdom, to be cleansed and to provide healing to all of us and in return the water yearns for our energy to vibrate with it. This is the ebb and flow of giving and receiving which once more needs to be unlocked.

In re-imagining something from the deepest past beyond memory, we must look within ourselves. There is no recorded history of the Sea Priestesses; we cannot look back into archaeological record and find traces of them for they existed before our time of record, their history is only our vague imaginings and inner knowing. To recreate their history in these pages I have taken the glimpses that remain and woven them together so that in my imagination and in my inner world their story makes sense to me.

As Above, so Below

The Sea Priestesses understood the connection between this blue planet and the stars, and they worked with the star system known as the Pleiades to divine the movements of the water on this planet. The Pleiades is a cluster star formation that can be seen in the winter in the Northern Hemisphere and the summer in the Southern Hemisphere. Its hot blue stars are easily seen with the naked eye. In Greek mythology the Pleiad(e)s were the seven daughters of Atlas and Pleione. Pleione was an Oceanid, a daughter of Oceanus and Tethys the Titan, who ruled the outer seas before being replaced by Poseidon. They were also known as the Atlantides.

The English translation of Pleiades is 'to sail' from the Greek, making the Pleione 'sailing queen' and her daughters were the 'the sailing ones.' They were named by the Greeks as the seven sisters, however there are actually nine bright stars that can be seen in the cluster. They are located in the constellation of Taurus and are among the nearest star clusters to Earth. The Greeks oriented the Parthenon to their rising and the Great pyramid at Giza was also orientated in this way. The element associated with the Pleiades is water and their position in the sky and the brightness of the stars was associated with the coming of the rains and the El-Nino phenomenon. Viewing and noting the brightness of these stars helped ancient farmers to know when to plant and when to harvest their crops. The Ancient Maya believe that their ancestors came from the Pleiades and settled the land known as Atlantis, as do many of the Indian tribes such as the Cherokee. These deep mythologies are the fragments of the past that we can piece together to find the lineage of the Sea Priestesses.

I believe that Atlantis actually existed many thousands of years ago and that our pre-history is much older than conventional science would have us believe. The stories of these ancient peoples have become our myths and legends of Gods and Goddesses. They allow us a glimpse into a world where the feminine and the earth were revered as sacred.

Atlantis of the Sea Priestesses

Homer and Plato give us written evidence of a place known as Atlantis, they also tell of its demise sinking beneath the ocean, destroyed by earthquakes and floods. The many tales of Atlantis tell of a beautiful place that fell into corruption and black magic, and where the population was destroyed when they tampered with the laws of nature for their own ends. It is now fairly well established that maybe 10,000 years ago the Earth was flooded and that life changed beyond recognition for its inhabitants. I believe 'though' that the Atlantis of these tales is much older and was maybe established 100,000 years ago and that the people who lived there were sailors and navigators. They lived in an advanced society where they used the natural forces of the Earth to power their homes and to create their society. They were sea people who travelled the blue planet making the ocean their home. They settled in Atlantis that is Antarctica today and set about navigating and mapping the planet. They had skills in mathematics, geophysics and map making. They mapped the Earth through the magnetic forces and natural spiritual pathways that today we know as ley lines or song lines. (*The Atlantis Blueprint,* Rand Flem-Ath and Colin Wilson)

It is the remnants of their talents in astronomy and mathematics that we may glimpse in our ancient past. Whether it is the Mayan Calendar, the building of the pyramids, the Nazca lines or the ancient spiritual paths to which we are reconnecting once more. Their society was deeply intuitive and they had learnt how to work with the natural environment in a way that allowed their society to flourish but which didn't harm the planet. They used the elements, earth, air, fire and water and combined it with their own life force and spirit to enhance and create their world. Their demise came 10,000 years ago when the forces of nature were so extreme that attempts to control them failed and most of what they had learnt died with them. The humans that survived them revered them in stories, which became myths and legends, and some of their ancient technologies were left behind and eventually utilised by the early hominids, whose matriarchal societies were based on the traditions they had imparted.

The ancient Sea Priestesses lived in this Altantean world. Theirs was a sacred duty and they were born with a natural intuitive nature that they then deepened through practice and the support of their sisterhood. As one of nine, the Sea Priestess's power was magnified and her intuition strengthened. They formed a web of communication, telepathically communicating with the planet and all its inhabitants, using the song lines on the planet in a similar way in which we use radio waves. Their purpose was to be receptive and passive, a channel of communication with the sentient planet on which they lived.

Sea Priestesses generally lived and worked together; they gained their emotional and personal support through the sisterhood. At an early age they would know they were destined for life as a Sea Priestess as their natural intuitive nature would evolve. They would then enter a sisterhood aged around twelve, replacing a sister who had passed. In this respect, sisterhoods often represented the many ages of women, through maiden to crone. The young girl would be tutored and mentored by the other women in her sisterhood. All were equal within the circle, and each would bring their own strength to the whole.

Ancient Ways of the Sea Priestesses

The ancient Sea Priestesses used the primal elements or the 'tattvas' to perform their practice. They used sound vibration (air), fire, water and earth. With this they combined the fifth element of spirit, their own and the life force of this planet, water, to communicate, heal and divine. Their practice was that of mantra (chanting), fully opening their etheric body and chakra energy points of which they had twelve, unlike our current seven. (*2012 and Beyond,* Diane Cooper). A further root chakra below the feet which allowed for deep communication with the planet; then three further chakras, one at the back of the crown, and the other two above the head. As fully enlightened beings they had full use of the twelve chakras. They would allow the divine and the spirit of the water to enter their etheric body so that they could sing her words to the people, connecting the planet and the stars, radiating the energy around the planet and out into the cosmos. In order to achieve this they became skilled at allowing, being passive and receptive. Like the moon in the night sky, they were reflective. In Chinese or Taoist thought they would be seen as Yin energy, described as mysterious, passive, soft, moist and chaotic. It is possible for us to also connect in this way and activate our own twelve chakras.

We can do this through activating our breath and connecting with the Earth and the water on a regular basis. We can also do this by chanting mantra, which is an ecstatic practice that clears and balances the etheric body.

The sound vibrations made during chanting, act on the inner and outer world and are a vehicle of transformation. In chanting sacred sounds or mantras the veil between the worlds can be lifted and we can enter other dimensions. A sacred sound vibration has the ability to transform matter. The vocalisation of the sound can alter reality. When we make sound it forms a wave that moves through matter. Sound at different frequency can cause items to shatter and break. We have all heard of the opera singer whose voice can shatter glass because it vibrates at a certain frequency. The Sea Priestesses used their voices to manipulate matter and to heal. They were able to communicate between dimensions and connect directly with the elementals. They were also able to change energy into any form and move objects by sound. They used the power of the 'word' in order to manifest their world. They understood the idea of cause and effect and how to influence through their thoughts and words. Their intention was for the highest good and for increasing communication between the planet and its inhabitants. They remained receptive and observed the interaction between the natural and elemental worlds.

In Fortune's book we hear the singing of the Sea Priestess as she stands at the water edge looking out to sea. Like the singing and calling of the mermaid her enchantment is through her voice.

'Impelled by what power I do not know, I rose and walked

towards her, and as I got close enough to see her face in the moonlight, I saw that it was not Morgan Le Fay at all, and that the eyes were strange and wide and inhuman, not even the eyes of the sea priestess, but that of the sea goddess herself. She raised her arms like the horns of Hathor and she sang to the moon and the sea' (*The Sea Priestess,* Dion Fortune pg 141*)*

The Sea Priestess would become the Goddess through embodying her and she would sing the world into being, giving form to the elements around her. At the sub atomic level all matter is the same. In the Bible the phrase from John 1.1 says *'In [the] beginning the Word was, and the Word was with God, and the Word was God.* (*Positive Magic,* Marion Weinstein*)* This is an ancient understanding of how thought manifests into form.

The Sea Priestess's magic was the power of transformation. In this manner she also performed her healing practice, chanting and working with the etheric body at a soul level in order to facilitate healing. Her words and vocalized sound had the ability to change the world and alter the universe at the quantum level. This was an extremely powerful state of being and for this reason the Sea Priestess only worked with the natural world and not against it or in manipulation of it, until of course the last days of Atlantis and we all know the outcome of this.

The Sea Priestess understood the sound vibrations of her words brought matter into existence. This is a concept that we are gradually seeing returning to modern consciousness popularised by such techniques as 'the Secret' and 'cosmic ordering'. There are two worlds; the world of form and the invisible world. The seen and the unseen world and it is in the interaction between these worlds where we see the rules of cause and effect. Quantum physics has given us an insight into the unseen world and has shown us that it behaves in quite extraordinary ways. The invisible world reflects our thoughts and our emotions. When we have an idea and we are emotionally attached to this idea, then it can manifest itself within the world of form or the seen world. The Sea Priestess did not see the world as fated or destined, rather she knew that fate drew from our belief about oneself and your role within the world. She knew that the invisible world would reflect back to what we put into it. So if we think the world a harmonious and peaceful place and that was what we declared it to be then that would be what was reflected back. She knew that each person was responsible for their own destiny and the thoughts they placed out into the world. Her role was to work with the invisible/unseen world so that she increased the positive and the healing energy of the planet.

The Sea Priestess and the Mermaid

In legend it is the mermaid's cry that takes sailors to their death, her sweet singing enchanting them out of this world into another. This is a remnant of the past passed down through myth and legend. Through the legends of the mermaid we can find clues to the work of the ancient Sea Priestesses. The mermaid is beautiful, she sings and her melodic voice lures men as she sits with a comb and mirror looking out to sea. She is of the sea and the Goddess, bare breasted she is a symbol of the All Mother. She is both the dark and the light, her beauty is treacherous just like the sea and she possesses the gift to see the future, grant wishes and heal humans. We see a remnant of their sisterhood in the myth of the sirens the spirits of beautiful women with the bodies of birds. They lived on stretches of rocky coast and lured boats onto dangerous rocks by enchanting the sailors with their song. This theme of enchantment through singing is also seen in the myth of the muses. The muses gave the gift of poetry and expression of creative thought. Each muse was responsible for gifting a separate literary, poetic or musical ability.

In the tales of the mermaid, the muses and the sirens, we see the tools and gifts of the Sea Priestess. She is the holder of the mirror; the mirror is the window into the soul. She can look into the hearts of all and see what is there to be discovered. In her use of the mirror she can look deep within herself, understanding her motivations and her true nature. It is within these reflections that she can understand her deepest desire. The voice and the singing of the Sea Priestess is her unique quality; in her song lie her dreams and her essential self.

Her song is sent out to the depths where it reverberates far and wide, capturing the beauty of the sound within the memory of the waters.

Each Sea Priestess enchants with her own song and this blends together with her sisters in a wonderful, all encompassing symphony. She sings of her desires, loves lost and won, of sisterhood, of wisdom and of inner knowing. Her song grows and changes with the years, unique and ever changing, taking on a life of its own. She sings of the beauty on the land and of the deep oceans. Her voice carrying on the air; she sings of loneliness, despair and the passing of the seasons. She sings the songs of her people, of their lives and loves. In her voice there is stillness and depth, crystalline remembrance. Her song creates and destroys, it brings joy and madness in equal measure for it belongs to her and her soul's journey, forever notated into the waters of the blue planet. To steal her song is to take her life: without it, she is less, parched, withered and denied. At her death her song is woven into the fabric of all the songs that have preceded it and is held in the collective memory. The Sea Priestess's song can still be heard as the ocean meets the land for those who choose to listen.

The Sea Priestess and the Veil

In describing Morgan le Fay, in Dion Fortune's *The Sea Priestess,* Wilfred explains how when she is in the outside world she remains veiled.

'Over the top of it one could just see her eyes, but no more. Apparently no one ever did see Miss Le Fay Morgan's face in the open street.' (*The Sea Priestess,* Dion Fortune, Pg 45)

Wearing a veil is an ancient symbol of the Sea Priestess because in wearing the veil she becomes otherworldly and is able to embody the Goddess. Today the veiling of women 'in my opinion' is often a way to hide the woman from the world and the eyes of other men. The Muslim tradition of women wearing the Burka is an evolution of this ancient Goddess tradition and is a practice where women should have choice; and in this respect there has been much derision of the practice particularly in the West where it has been seen as a patriarchal control of women. In respect of where women are required to wear a veil in order to satisfy male control it is a deeply disrespectful practice; however' where it is the woman's choice it can liberating. For the Sea Priestess, the wearing of the veil is symbolic of the Priestess's connection with the divine. In opening herself to embody the Goddess, her veiling allowed for a state of altered consciousness where she can remove herself from the mundane world in order to facilitate communication with the divine.

When a woman covers her face with a veil, it can allow her to enter the world of spirit and for her to embody the Goddess within. The practice of using a veil during meditation and ceremony can deepen the experience for the individual. *(Priestess of Avalon, Priestess of the Goddess, Kathy Jones)*

Connecting to the Waters of Life

In order to understand the ancient ways of the Sea Priestess you will undertake an exercise to connect yourself to the divine waters of life. You will do this by following a practice of the ancient Sea Priestess, which I have channelled through meditation. You will chant using ancient Sanskrit words; however you could just as easily use English or your own native language to do so. You are utilising an ancient language to imbue the words with the power of generations that have spoken them before you in a sacred way. However if you are uncomfortable using Sanskrit then you can use the English translation given. You will also do this exercise veiled in order to experience how this feels. Notice if it alters your perception and the way in which you feel before during and after. You may wish to note this in your journal. Quite often our experience can be coloured by past life experiences and it can take courage to place yourself in the heart of this women's mystery. Experiment with the mantra and the sounds your body makes. Allow yourself to make it your own. Note changes in your perception of the outside world, if any. In performing this practice you will remove yourself from ordinary reality and you will experience change in your inner and outer world. Be prepared for these changes and treat yourself with care. Make sure to drink plenty of pure natural water and if at anytime you are uncomfortable then please stop and take time and care of yourself. These exercises seem very simple but they are very powerful and you need to give yourself time and allow yourself to move into and out of them gently.

Mantra Exercise

Om Chandra Samudra (infinity moon sea) this mantra connect us to the waters of life and the reflective and opening nature of the moon. You can utilise this mantra to allow yourself to connect to our blue planet, the moon and the tides and to connect to the waters of life. This exercise is beautiful sat in the moonlight by a body of water, however it can also be done at any time when you wish to connect yourself to water or the moon or to experience this ancient practice. It is a very powerful mantra that will connect you to the infinity of all; and as such it should be given the respect deserved and chanted in a sacred way.

Covering your head with a light material or veil, ground and centre yourself by imagining you are connected to the ground beneath you and the sky above at your heart. Take a seated pose with legs crossed and hands resting on your knees with the first finger and thumb touching each other. This hand placing or 'Mudra' represents inner knowledge. Start to take some deep breaths, allow your breath to completely fill your lungs. Breathe into the womb space, the sacral chakra and imagine this chakra as a spinning orange ring, opening more with each breath. Then taking a breath in, on the out breath chant 'Om' then breathe in again and this time on the out breath say 'Chandra', then breathe once more and on the out breath say 'Samudra'. Repeat this sequence three times and in three sets, resting between each set, allowing your breath to return to its natural rhythm until you have chanted the mantra nine times in total. Allow your breathing to settle and sit quietly for a moment before bringing your attention back to the sacral chakra and allowing the energy to settle and the chakra to close down fully. Remove your veil and give yourself time to come back into the mundane world. Write about how you felt and how the experience was. As you become more experienced you can work up to nine sets of nine. This mantra is a healing mantra and works with the unseen world to deepen your connection to the planet and the natural forces upon it

Another version of the mantra is Om Ma Chandra, which is a blessing to the moon and the mother Goddess who is 'Mari' in this chant. This mantra or invocation can be sang or chanted.

Om Ma Chandra
Om Ma Mari
Om Ma Chandra
Om Ma Mari
Blessings of the mother
From the moon and the Sea
Blessing of the mother
Divine divinity

As with the other mantra above you can sing this whilst

veiled. The repetitive singing of the mantra will take you to a place of ecstasy where your mind quiets and you can find your inner wisdom.

Notes

Notes

5

The Song Lines

The Aboriginal peoples of the world keep the dreamtime and the song lines. Those who still know how to sing the world into existence keep the secrets and the mystery. In modern times the concept is beyond the consciousness of most people. The Shaman of South America and the aboriginals of Australia understand that the Earth is covered in song lines (or ley lines as they have become known in the West). These lines are the energetic veins of the Earth and criss cross the land marking the ancient pathways of her peoples. The song lines tell the story of creation and they reveal the nature of this planet. The Sea Priestesses of ancient times worked with these energy lines and sang the world into existence. They understood that thought precedes form and used the energy of these lines to communicate with the water and this sentient planet.

The Sea Priestess works with the energies of these song lines in her healing practice and to tune into the heartbeat of the Earth. The song lines speak to her of the ancestors, of the changing of the season, of the past, the present and the moment. She can see the threads that weave the world and she understands that as she moves through the land she leaves these threads behind her as well. To work in harmony with the land and the sea, it is necessary to know how to listen to the song lines, and for the Sea Priestess to know how her own song mingles with that of the land into which she journeys.

I remember when I first arrived in Australia, this strange land not only looked different from my homeland but it felt different too. For six months I wandered around like someone with lead boots attached to their feet. I found not just the heat but also the energy of the land itself sapping my strength. In a period of a few months I gained almost a stone in weight. Adjusting to the energy of this new land was exhausting yet immensely satisfying when I worked with it. When I adjusted my diet and my exercise routine and when I walked and sat on the land, and listened to the earth and what it had to tell me. The manner in which I experienced time changed, everything slowed and I needed to slow with it. I could no longer rush around but had to listen to my inner voice telling me that it was OK to go to bed at 9pm and get up at 5am, that it was OK to graze rather than try and eat large meals as I had done in the UK. Attuning myself allowed me to experience what she offered and by listening to the song lines of the land I experienced the vibrant colour and feel of the place with all my senses. Listening to the song lines I used all of my senses, noticing, and listening to my intuition.

I found that when I returned to the UK, I felt the energy more keenly than I had done before I moved. I started noticing things that previously I had ignored. Ancient sites attracted me, and I explored the countryside near my new home. The joy of being outside and walking the land (regardless of the weather) was a pleasure. My greatest enjoyment still comes from walking the coastal paths, near to where I live and hearing the sea singing to the land. I began to resent being cooped up inside as I came to understand that this was where I could communicate with the divine within and without.

Since returning I have travelled all over the world and walking the land of the place is an essential part of the journey. Connecting me with the people, the land and the divine spirit of the place.

The song lines interconnect each place; each line has a unique energy signal or song that keeps the secrets of the peoples who have lived there and their joys and sadness. When you travel and tune in, you add your own energy to the place. It is important to ask the Earth and the ancestors of the land if you can sing with them and join your voice. It is vital to respect the land and the sea. The Earth is alive and her voice is there to be heard for those who listen. Where the sea meets the land you can hear the song of the sea, mixing with the Earth songs and rejoicing as the songs are carried around the world and held in the memory of the water.

To listen to the song lines, the Sea Priestess needs to walk the land regardless of where she lives, town, city or country, you can explore the songs of your land by getting out and walking on the Earth, even if it is covered in concrete. As a practice it is important to really get to know where you live. I am always amazed by how many people do not know the place where they live, its no wonder there is so much disconnection from the Earth.

To know the land in which you live means to walk it. You cannot know it by travelling by car, bus or train or even bicycle. When you walk the land you walk it with purpose.

Your intention is to feel the energy of the place and to listen and notice. It is an exercise in noticing. It is much easier in the first instance to listen to the Earth in a familiar place, where you feel at home and where your energy signature and 'your song line' is already strong. When you feel connected to your home and the area around it, then you can move your attention to listening to the ocean and how it meets with the land and reverberates the song lines around the planet. You can also travel to other places and be amazed by what you feel and how your life changes as a result.

For the Sea Priestess, the song line is one of the most important concepts for her to learn. She sings her world into creation and that singing leaves an indelible legacy on the Earth. It is how the world was created and how she experiences it. Rather than being in a one-dimensional world the Sea Priestess exists within four conscious realities. These four realities are spirit, soul, mind and body. She can operate at all four levels of consciousness simultaneously, moving effortlessly between them. In chapter two we learnt a simple grounding exercise that is the first stage in listening and noticing the Earth. Whilst walking the land you should do the grounding exercise as often as possible. Take time to just be; sitting or standing outside, expand your awareness out into the world. Notice the sounds you hear, feel the air and the elements on your skin. What do you smell? What does the air taste like? *(Priestess of Avalon, Priestess of the Goddess, Kathy Jones)*

Tuning into the Song Lines

To tune into the song lines we are going to perform an

expanded version of the grounding exercise you learnt in chapter two.

Stand with your feet evenly spaced about a foot apart, put your hands on your hips. Take five deep breaths, make sure that you fill your lungs as much as you can, you can breathe through the nose or the mouth, whichever feels more comfortable. On the exhale make sure that you exhale through your mouth making an audible sound as you do so. This breath is deeply relaxing and eliminating.

After the deep breaths, close your eyes and breathe normally but deeply. Listen to your breath as you inhale and exhale, (if you begin to feel dizzy or disorientated open your eyes for a moment) imagine the breath circulating throughout your body. Feel the oxygen reaching all the parts of your body, moving through your circulatory system re-energising it on the in breath and detoxifying it on the out breath. After a few minutes of just breathing, imagine your life force energy circulating around your body, moving down through your root chakra (the base of your spine), down through your feet into the ground below you. See that energy making its way down through the land, through the earth, through the rock and stone and the sub layers of earth down deep into the Earth's core. Here your energy meets with the energies of the Earth mother, feel her nurturing, loving energy mixing with your own. Feel your feet firmly rooted and planted into the ground like the roots of a tree. Draw the energy of Mother Earth up through those roots into your body and feel her energy mixing with your life force. Feel the energy in your heart.

Then, moving with your breathing on the in breath draw

the energy up from the Earth to your crown then on the out-breath send the energy back down through the heart, through the root down into the Earth, do this for at least three breaths. Then take the breath higher each time out into the sky, each time bringing it back down to the Earth. Connect with your mother star and then bring this energy down into the Earth. Feel yourself completely connected from the stars to the earth below. The energy radiating out from your heart chakra.

When you feel completely connected allow your breath to settle. Listen to the Earth below your feet see if you can sense the energy lines and listen to what you feel. Expand your awareness out into the world and listen.

When you are ready return your awareness back to your breathing and open your eyes. Try this exercise in many different places, record what you notice and feel.

Notes

Notes

6

Journeying with the Moon

The way of the Sea Priestess requires those who undertake the practice to have an intimate relationship with the moon and its phases. You work with the moon as it moves through its different aspects and you reflect upon the effects in both the natural world and on your own body.

The moon's gravitational pull on the planet affects the water that flows on it and the water that flows through our bodies. The phases of the moon mark the passing of time and the solar calendar we now use was not the one used by our ancestors who marked the time through a lunar calendar. This thirteen-month year is the feminine year and reflects the movement of the moon from new, through to full, and then dark. The phases of the moon impact our bodies and emotional state, as the tide ebbs and flows with the moon so do we. This is true for all people but for women the effect is even more marked, for our menstrual cycle is often linked to the moon phase, particularly where the woman lives close to nature. Each phase of the moon is associated with a Goddess and also with a season. In the practice we move through the phases so we can attune ourselves to our internal energies.

During your practice it is a useful exercise to keep a moon diary. In this diary you can keep track of your menstrual cycle, moods and energy levels. This is an important exercise even if you are no longer bleeding as you can attune yourself to nature's natural rhythms. The moon cycle around the Earth takes approximately twenty-eight days which is the same amount of time as a woman's menstrual cycle and when you live close to nature the two can become harmonic with each other. Your blood and hormonal cycles follow the ebb and flow of the moon from new through to full and dark.

In the cycle of the new moon, oestrogen increases which leads to ovulation and the most fertile period at the full moon. Then as the moon wanes, progesterone dominates the hormones and bleeding begins during the dark period of the moon. When your body is out of sync with nature you can find that your life force becomes diminished and that symptoms such as Premenstrual syndrome can become aggravated. The modern world does not encourage women to honour their cycles, as was, and is common in ancient cultures; then women would shut themselves away to bleed, dream and foster their innate creativity.

At a personal level I know what it is to distance yourself from your natural cycle in order to feed the demands that the modern world places upon you. In 2001, aged thirty-four I had an endometrial ablation, this is a surgical procedure that burns away that part of the uterus, the endometrial lining that is the part of the womb that is shed when you have your menses and is the lining that builds up during the month ready to nurture the embryo if you were to become pregnant during that cycle. I had suffered from excessive bleeding for a number of years prior to this procedure and had become quite anaemic, however, although my bleeding was heavy I had no underlying condition. With a busy job and two young children to care for, I would be lying if I said that having my periods taken away hadn't removed one huge hassle from me at that stage in my life. I no longer needed to purchase sanitary protection or have the embarrassment of the flooding that went with my heavy period, and as a worker I no longer needed the down time that my period had demanded of me. Certainly no one pressured me to have the procedure but then neither did anyone describe to me other ways of dealing with the situation. I did not honour in myself the deep inner connection that would be lost by abruptly ending my menses. As I have moved towards peri-menopause, I have found that my natural barometer for self-health and inner knowing isn't there to guide me and I feel a deep sense of loss. This is not to indicate that this procedure or hysterectomy should not be sought, there are valid medical reasons for both which can distinctly outweigh the disadvantages. However, I do believe that by not honouring my own body and its processes, and conforming to the accepted patriarchal working world, I did not allow my body its own self healing which could well have achieved a similar result in my case where there was no underlying disease.

'Our lady is also the moon, called of some Selene, of others, Luna, but by the wise Levanah, for therein is contained the number of her name. She is the ruler of the tides of flux and reflux. The waters of the great sea answer unto her, likewise the tides of all earthly seas, and she ruleth the nature of women.' (*The Sea Priestess* Dion Fortune Pg 166)

A woman's moon time is a time of magic and inner power, a time where she can release those things that are no longer working and dream into being those things that are yet to come. Ancient people knew this and women would generally segregate themselves allowing the older non-bleeding women or men to take care of domestic and work chores. Women would enter a moon lodge and would gather together to reconnect to the divine mother, replacing and releasing the old energies for the new fertility to come. In this sacred space women were the carriers of abundance and fertility. In following the cycle of the moon, women acknowledged their connection to all of nature and allowed their natural intuitive selves.

Even if we are unable to segregate ourselves like the women of old, then we can acknowledge where we are in our cycle and in doing so we can honour the sacred traditions and open our intuitive inner knowing. As the moon causes the tides to ebb and flow and reflects the life-giving blood (her waters of this Earth) we can follow our own ebb and flow through our blood. In doing so we acknowledge the inner receptive nature of ourselves, we trust our body, our emotions and our intuition to lead us along the path of our lives.

Journeying with the Moon

As a Sea Priestess you will journey with the moon as you deepen your practice. You will become instinctively aware of the phases and astrological houses though which the moon travels and build your relationship with her. It will be a different journey for everyone but one which will follow the natural pattern of life and the ebb and flow of the planet and its waters. You will find yourself reflected in the patterns that she shows you. Like the tide you will have your low and your high points but by tracing these patterns in yourself you can find your truth.

Keeping a Moon Diary

An important part of this practice is keeping a moon diary. A moon diary is a diary of your inner world. It is where you journal your moods, your menstrual cycle and your emotional state. You can purchase diaries that will tell you what phase the moon is in and in what astrological phase. However you can just as easily keep a journal and download an ephemeris or the moon phases from the internet. You should aim to write in your diary every day, even if it's as simple as describing your mood and what cycle/house the moon is in.

E.g. 4th May – New moon in Aries – energetic

Of course if you spend more time then you will get a better picture of your inner world and how the moon impacts on it. In writing your journal you can also get a deeper understanding of your own nature.

Below you will find the phases of the moon and then the meanings given for each moon in each of the twelve houses, which you can utilise within your moon diary. As with all of these exercises, you can use the accepted meanings, however you will develop greater inner wisdom by also trying to ascribe your own meanings because they will uncover the deeper workings of your inner psyche. You can then work backwards and understand how the planets and the phases impact you personally.

The Moon as Mirror

The moon is a mirror: it has no light of its own but reflects the light of the sun. The Sea Priestess understands the power of the moon as she also understands the power of the mirror. In the mirror the Sea Priestess can look into her own eyes and understand the mystery of her soul; she can divine the future, and work with all that is, was and is yet to come. The moon represents the shadow side of the sun: it lights the night where we can meet our shadow selves and come face to face with our fears; as the Sea Priestess can when she sees her own reflection.

We cannot look directly at the sun so it is the moon that allows us to see its brightness. As we cannot directly see ourselves but must look into the mirror in order to see within.

Phases of the Moon

The phases of the moon are dependent on the moon's position in relation to the Earth and the sun. The moon has no light of its own but reflects the light of the sun back to Earth. The time it takes for the moon to rotate on its axis is the same time it takes for it to make one revolution around the Earth, so when we look up into the night sky we will only ever see the same face of the moon wherever we are on Earth.

The phase of the moon is the portion of the moon that we can see lit up by the sun, dependant on the angle between the Earth and the sun. Each phase of the moon is associated with a Goddess and also with a season in the practice and as we move through the phases we can tune ourselves to our internal energies.

New Moon

This is where the sun and moon are together in the same sign of the zodiac, it is generally notated as:

because no light is reflected at this time. We associate this phase of the moon with new beginnings and the time of Imbolc, which we associate with the Goddess as Coventina of the wells and springs. The quality of this period is that of the child, a time of innocence and naivety. We work with the moon in this phase as a time to initiate. The new moon is a time of new beginnings when we can work with the natural world to discover new ways of being and doing.

Waxing Crescent Moon

This is where we start to see the moon appear on the western horizon and we see a small glimmer of light beginning to grow, appearing first as a thin crescent. This is a time of growth, reflected in the season of Spring Equinox and we work with the Goddess as Sabrina of the rivers, the life giving arteries of the land. The quality of this time is of energy and the starting of projects. We work with the moon in this phase to expand. This is the time where we have the energy to do all of the things we have been planning and where getting up and out into the world seems effortless.

First Quarter

The moon is now a full crescent in the night sky and the quality is sensual, reflected in the season of Beltane and the Goddess Aphrodite. Change is rapid and we can find ourselves caught up in the whirlwind of life. This is a time when we find we are full of energy and our sex drive can be at its peak. We are sensuous and achieving orgasm during lovemaking is almost guaranteed.

Waxing Gibbous - Half Moon

The sun and moon are now at 90° and form a square to each other. The moon appears to be half-light and half dark. The energy of this time reflects this duality, as the moon begins to move towards its waning half. This is a time of evaluation and is reflected in the season of Litha and the Goddess Sulis. This is a time where the sun also reaches its zenith.

Full Moon

The sun and moon are now at the same degree but in opposite signs of the zodiac and the moon fully reflects the light of the sun. It is notated as:

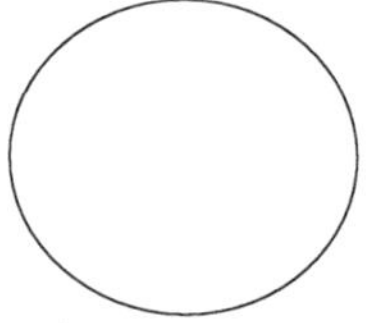

This is a time of fulfillment and reflection. At the full moon we can see what we have achieved and accomplished. The gravity of the moon is now at its strongest and our emotions are heightened and we are at our most sensitive. The full moon is a magical time when we see the fruition of our dreaming. It is also a time associated with madness and where psychologically people can be vulnerable. Here we look into the mirror to see our reflection. We can see the Goddess of the centre within and without.

Last Quarter

The moon rises later and it starts to turn away from the sun, this is the time to review what has been; acknowledging the changes we have experienced. It is represented by the time of Lammas, this is the time of the harvest and the Goddess as Boann in our wheel. This is a time to give thanks and express our gratitude for all that we have and all that we are.

Waning Gibbous Moon

The moon is again at 90° but now it is turning away from the sun. Again we are at a time of duality represented by Autumn Equinox and Yemanya. We can feel the change in ourselves and in nature as we look inward rather than out into the world.

Waning Crescent Moon

When the moon is in waning crescent this is the time when we can often see the moon during daylight hours as it rises in the early morning. This is a time to examine our internal world, to go into ourselves and find our inner knowing. We enter the cave of the mother. A time associated with Samhain and the Goddess of transformation, Vivienne. We enter the cave to begin our dreaming.

Dark Moon

Now the moon is dark and we can no longer see it in the night sky. This is the dreamtime, when we are at our most intuitive and where our inner world takes precedence. At the dark moon we can look inward and examine those parts of our lives that aren't working. We can discover the shadow self. This is the time to look at those soul parts of you that are wounded, fractured or that need tending. This is a time associated with Yule and with Sedna. This is the dreamtime.

The Moon in all Twelve Houses

As well as the phase of the moon, the moon also moves from sign to sign in the twelve houses of the zodiac. This influence can be felt most keenly at the new and the full moon. The moon is reflective and as such reflects back to us the energies of the sign in which it's placed. It takes about two and a half days for the moon to move through each house. We can utilise the energies presented at each astrological phase to plan projects or even plant our garden. If you are a healer or are looking to harness healing energies, then being aware of where the moon is in relation to the zodiac can help you to work with, rather than against, the natural energies present.

It is a useful exercise to find out which sign the moon was in at your time of birth as it can be a good indicator of your inner nature and the way in which you interact socially with others. This is particularly true for women, as the placement of your moon can help unlock the desires within you, leading to inner fulfillment. In order to find your moon sign you will need to know your time and place of birth. There are many online programs available, which will tell you your moon sign. Below are the generally accepted meanings for the moon in each of its astrological placing. As you record your moods and feelings at each phase of the moon you will develop your own interpretation and these will not necessarily be the same as the more generalised meanings.

Moon in Aries

Aries is in the first house and this is the most energetic sign. Its fiery nature can give us the initiating energy that we need to begin. The moon in Aries will give us the spurt of energy that we require but it is short lived and burns itself out quickly. The moon in Aries calls us to look at how we present ourselves to the outside world.

Moon in Taurus

This is the moon that highlights our need for security and that enhances our love of food and our home comforts. It can bring forth our deepest insecurities and make us question ourselves. Take time out, pamper yourself and look to your deep inner desires and find a way to fulfill them while the moon is in this aspect. Any project begun should be of a practical and stable nature. If you wish to get your finances in order, a Taurus moon will help with the process.

Moon in Gemini

The moon in the third house emphasises groups and companionship. This lively aspect can bring joy to group endeavors and encourages communication of all sorts. If you have something difficult to communicate to another, a Gemini moon can help this communication. Be wary though as under this moon you could start too many things and then not have the energy to complete them.

Moon in Cancer

The moon is in its exaltation in Cancer, here we find the deepest love reflected in the way that we approach our family and our home life. Here the moon is mother and we can use this energy to nurture others and ourselves. If you feel in need of some inner care, the moon in Cancer is a perfect time to treat or pamper yourself. If you need to make changes in your home or environment now is the time to do so.

Moon in Leo

The moon is in its detriment in Leo that rules the fiery sun. It can bring out our doubts about self-image and the face we show to the world. But it can also inspire our creativity and playfulness. This the moon of the artist, and we can all utilise its energies to appreciate our own and others creativity. Now is the time to paint, to play music and to fall in love with our creative nature.

Moon in Virgo

Practicality and attention to detail is highlighted when the moon is in Virgo. It can reflect our most pedantic natures, but is a great moon under which to start projects that need practical and analytical attention. This is a resourceful time where you can analyse and determine.

Moon in Libra

Here the moon is justice and fairness. All aspects relating to fair treatment and the way in which we approach our relationships with others is highlighted. This is the time to share and to establish connection. It can be a time when we may wish to evaluate our friendships and dealings with others. If you are involved in any form of legal dispute or something where you need a fair outcome, the moon, in Libra is a time to resolve these issues.

Moon in Scorpio

Here there could be self-deception and a need to withdraw from the world. This is the time to open yourself and get in touch with your inner world. It can be a time to listen to your intuition and to let go and allow healing of inner wounds. This can be a wonderful time to enter a retreat or to heal inner issues.

Moon in Sagittarius

This moon favour's travel and the pursuit of educational opportunities, this is a time where we look outside ourselves and interact with others. A good time to start an educational course or to plan a trip.

Moon in Capricorn

The Capricorn moon allows for the practical application of skills and talents to enable us to further our goals. Now is the time to implement the practical actions that will attain our goals. This is the doing moon.

Moon in Aquarius

This moon is the humanitarian moon that turns our concern for self, outward to the needs of others. We can feel compassion and love for our fellow human beings. Science and technology projects are favoured, as are all charitable pursuits. This is the moon of future trends and activities. An avid fan of Sci-fi may find they have a moon in Aquarius.

Moon in Pisces

This moon can cause us to withdraw and to feel isolated from others and we can be tempted to overindulge in food or substances. However, harnessed creatively, we can be inspired to create deep and meaningful works of art, music and poetry.

Ritual and Ceremony

The many exercises in this book require you to create ceremony to honour yourself and your cycle and now you have started keeping a moon diary you can see how closely your body is in tune with nature. At the end of this chapter you will find ceremonies to perform at the new, full and dark moon and these will allow you to harmonise further with these natural rhythms. If you feel out of harmony in your body then these ceremonies can be helpful in balancing your hormones and your body.

It is important for us to respect our bodies and to understand where we are in our own cycle. We need to listen deeply. If we continue our normal routines and do not respect our bodies then we can become tired, irritable and our emotional states become out of balance. We need to find time for rest, meditation and allow others to take on more of the outside chores in our lives, such as work and the care of children, particularly when we are in our bleeding state. Doing so will allow for introspection and will mean that in the remainder of our lives we are true to ourselves and therefore more productive. Giving ourselves this timeout can seem like an insurmountable obstacle in a world that expects us to be superwomen, 24/7, three hundred and sixty five days of the year, and yet to not do so means that we can deny our own mystery as a creative power-force. This is not our unique feminine state.

You will be undertaking ritual as part of your practice and using sacred objects to place your intention from thought into form. The word 'ritual' can seem quite daunting, but in actuality it just means taking time out from your busy routine to connect with the divine and yourself in a practical way. Ritual is something that has been lost to many in the modern world and yet it can anchor you. You are communicating to the universe that you are following a new practice. This will require leaving behind your old self and opening your heart to the new. You will state that you wish to honour the changes you are going to be making in your life. You will work with the Goddess energy of the season and ask for guidance and help in making these changes.

For all the rituals in this book, if you can be outside and ideally near the sea then the power of the ritual will be enhanced. However if you are unable, or live a large distance from the sea, then you can just as easily perform the ritual in the comfort of your own home.

Sacred Space and Objects

When you perform a ceremony in nature, whether by the sea or on the land, then you are already working within sacred space, as all of nature is sacred. You may wish to state to the universe and to yourself that you are doing something that is outside of the ordinary. A space or an object becomes sacred when we give it meaning beyond the ordinary.

In your home it's useful to have a space where you can perform your practice that is outside of the ordinary, you can do this by changing the energy of the space. Although this sounds complicated, in reality it is very easy. Find an area of your home that is easily accessible and unlikely to be disturbed by pets or children. It may be a corner of a room or even a shelf. Within this space you can keep objects and items that have special meaning. (If you live in a very small space with children and animals you may have to put your items away when not using them). The meaning of these items should be special to you and could derive from the time of the year, your moon cycle or just be an object that resonates with you. If you have a statue or image of the Goddess you can also place it within this space.

This object will then remind you of your connection with the divine both without and within. It will become an aide memoire to your spiritual practice. It allows you to look at the object anew and discover deeper meaning within the ordinary. It alters the subconscious mind so that on looking at the objects and entering the space, you know that you have entered a space that is out of the ordinary. It is special and sacred to you.

You will use a chalice or cup for many of the ceremonies and exercises in the book. So this cup or chalice will become one of your special sacred objects that you will keep in this space. This cup or chalice will become the grail, the symbol of your innate wisdom contained in your womb and your feminine intuition. You will bless your chalice as a magical tool for use throughout the time of the practice. If you don't already have a chalice then you will need to acquire one. The chalice should resonate with you and you should only use it for your practice. You will use the chalice for blessing, anointing and scrying as you move along your path.

'As the custom was, a great bowl was carried in and placed in the centre of the table; it was not of the bright gold such as we know today, but the pale aurichalcum that was used in Atlantis, and it was richly wrought with the waves of the sea…I knew that this was a sacred cup, the prototype of the grail.' (*The Sea Priestess,* Dion Fortune pg 113)

To make your chalice a sacred object you will need to start by collecting together the things you require for the ritual, you will need:

- Water – sea if possible or otherwise salted water
- Spring water for drinking
- Incense (white sage or something else which is purifying)

- A white candle
- Beach sand

Plus, of course, the chalice itself.

Start by grounding and centering yourself. Stand with your feet firmly planted on the ground. Breathe deeply and imagine yourself rooted to the Earth. Feel the energies of the Earth coming up through your feet until they reach your heart. Then send your energies out and upwards to the heavens until you reach your mother star and then bring this star fire back to the Earth, drawing it back down through your crown and into your heart. Let this heart energy fill you and expand outwards around you. When you feel centered in yourself you may then wish to ask the Goddess to be present with you in the space. When speaking to the Goddesses, do so in a respectful way, asking them if they wish to be there with you. Ask for their qualities to be available to you and try to include those things, for which you are thankful. Within this particular exercise, ask that you may set your intentions clearly for your practice.

Once grounded and centered you will begin with making the chalice a sacred object. Set up a space with the chalice in the centre and the elements in the directions: earth to the North, then air to the East, fire to the South and water to the West. However, if you wish, you can place the element in the direction in which it feels most right for you. Light your candle and your incense. You will then pass the chalice through the elements and at each element state your intention. Below is a guide but it is very important that the words are your own and reflect your own intention and most importantly the highest good of all.

Taking your beach sand fill the chalice with the sand and say a blessing:

'Let this sand symbolise and ground my intention when using this chalice.'

Then pass the chalice through the smoke of the incense:

'As I pass this chalice through the element of air let it be used with wisdom.'

Then pass through the candle flame:

'Let fire energise my use of this chalice so that I can know my true purpose'

Then finally fill with the seawater, if you are at the beach then allow the tide to run over your chalice washing it with the water:

'As Sea Priestess let me use my chalice to open the pathways of the inner world, to allow my emotional expression and love to flow.'

Finally fill the chalice with drinking water and offer to the Goddess as a symbol of your intention to follow this pathway. Blessing the water as appropriate, drink from your chalice. Then, thanking the Goddess, give a blessing out loud and ground the energy of the ritual, either by placing your hands together in prayer or touching the ground.

Your chalice is now blessed as a sacred object to you and you should use it only within your practice.

Moon Rituals

You will now begin your journey with the moon and below you will find a ceremony for each phase. Follow the moon for a lunar month and perform the ceremony dependant on what phase the moon is in when you start.

New Moon Ceremony

Choose a time and a place where you will not be disturbed and preferably where you can see the moon. If you can perform your ceremony near the sea or a body of water it will allow you to fully experience the energies present, however it is not necessary to do the ceremony either during the evening or by the sea, and the practicalities may make this difficult. You do not need to be a bleeding woman to perform this ceremony, as those of us who are peri-menopausal or who have reached menopause and beyond can benefit from honouring natures cycles and Mother Earth's phases and in doing so become more in tune with our bodies and the effect the moon has upon us. It is, however, important that the moon is in a new phase. As with any ceremony or ritual that forms part of the Sea Priestess practice, it is important that the words and energies used reflect your own needs and inner experience so what is given below is for inspirational purposes only.

At the time of the new moon you will create new conditions and/or bring new things into your life. This is a time in a woman's cycle when she is in an oestrogen phase and where her body is preparing itself for ovulation and the new life that may result. The womb lining is thickening and you can feel at your most energetic and it can be a good time to really move forward energetically with creative or physical pursuits.

As you have done in the previous exercises, you will begin by setting up your space with the items you need; grounding and centering yourself and then inviting the seasonal Goddess of this aspect into the space. For this ceremony, set up a central altar with a representation of each element e.g. a candle for fire, sand for earth, incense for air and water. Place your chalice in the centre, filled with drinking water. Place onto this central altar representations of things you wish to see grow in your life. If these are not things but feelings and emotions then state them out loud and place them energetically into the space. You will also be making a vision board so collect together pictures and other representations of those things you would like to see grow and a large piece of cardboard for sticking these images onto; this will become your vision board. For example if you wish to have more joy in your life then collect pictures from magazines or other items that represent what joy means to you.

Sit within the space you have ceremonially created, close your eyes and allow yourself to dream about those things you wish to see grow. After you have done this, spend the time taking the images and sticking them to your board, and as you do so, imagine these images becoming part of your daily reality. When you have finished spend some time just being within this sacred space you have created. At the end of your ceremony say a prayer of thanks to the Goddess for being in your space and drink the water from your chalice, thanking the Goddess for the gift of water.

Full Moon Ceremony

The full moon ceremony that you are going to perform will be a ritual of thanks and gratitude for all that you have in your life. The full moon signifies fulfillment of your dreams and it is the time when the moon is at its most reflective. It is a time to take stock of what has been achieved and to give thanks. This is the time during a woman's cycle when she is at her most fertile and conception of new life happens. Her womb lining has thickened providing a home for the newly fertilized egg she has released at ovulation. For the Earth, the sea tides are at they're highest and the Earth reflects back our own internal processes. Here connection is complete and we are at one with nature and ourselves.

As you did for the new moon ceremony, collect together the directional objects for your central altar and place your chalice at the centre filled with drinking water. You will also need some beads and thread to make a gratitude bracelet. Create your sacred space by grounding and centering and then calling the directional Goddess into the space. Then, as before, take some time to meditate on what it is in your life that you are grateful for. When you are ready, taking a bead, one at a time, begin to thread your bracelet and with each bead state out loud what it is that you are grateful for. Make a knot between each bead that you thread. When you have finished tie the bracelet onto your wrist. Say a prayer of thanks to the Goddess for being with you in this sacred space and take a drink from your chalice. Thank the Goddess for the gift of water. Wear your bracelet between now and the dark moon to remind you each day of those things in your life for which you are grateful.

Dark Moon Ceremony

The dark moon is a time of release, as a bleeding woman it may be that you are actually menstruating at this phase of the moon. In ancient cultures the women bled onto the Earth, releasing as she symbolically gave back to mother nature all she had received during the preceding month. You may wish to do this as part of your ceremony if appropriate. That a woman could bleed and yet not be wounded or dying was a great source of power in past times and a strong link between women and the Earth Goddess. These are the blood mysteries and they teach us to remember that we all come from the Great Mother and that her blood, our blood is a healing blood, able to bring forth life and provide nourishment. Menstruation today is often regarded by women as a nuisance and as something that needs to be cleaned up and dealt with, a minor inconvenience that must be ignored so that 'normal' life can be resumed, yet as bleeding women we know that at this time we feel different and have a natural tendency to want to withdraw and to go within, exploring our inner world. This is a time of deep creativity of being able to dream and of accessing our innate intuitive nature.

The ceremony that you will create for the dark moon should be performed during this phase and, if possible when it's dark. If the ceremony is being performed in daylight hours then try and create a darkened space. The space should be set up so that it has a dark, womb-like feeling. An ideal scenario would be to pitch a small tent on a quiet beach where you can then perform the ceremony. Take note of health and safety though when you are using candles, by placing them in a container with the naked flame protected. Set up your altar in the same way as the preceding two ceremonies, ground and centre and invite the Goddess energy into the space. Taking some deep breaths allow yourself space to just sit and be. As thoughts come into your mind, allow them, but let them pass like clouds floating by. This is a special time just for you, a time when you can be relaxed, when there is nothing to achieve, nothing is required from you. Savour these moments of nothingness, sitting within the womb of the mother at this, the dark moon time, when she will take all from you that is no longer needed. As you sit, allow yourself to think of those things that have occurred in your life over the past months or years that you no longer need, that you would like to shed, along with the lining of your/her womb. Allow your emotions to flow. If you feel like laughing, laugh, if you feel like crying, then do so. This is your space; she will take all that you give her. If you are angry beat a pillow, scream, shout into it, and release all of the emotion that resides within you whatever that emotion may be, without judgment about whether it is right or wrong. Whatever you are feeling is right and should be allowed in this space. When you have finished sit or lie down and imagine yourself held in the womb of the mother Goddess. You may feel like resting or even sleeping for a while. When you are ready, thank the Goddess for this time and take a drink from your chalice, thanking her for the waters and the blood that flows and for emotional release.

Start your practice

Keeping your moon diary throughout you can now begin, dependant on the season

Notes

Notes

7

Samhain and Yule

Samhain is the old Celtic New Year where the veil between the inner and outer world is thin. Here we can commune with our ancestors and gestate the ideas and creative projects that we wish to see come to fruition. You will journey into the dreamtime into the stillness that holds the promise of the new with Vivienne, rest in the lake/cauldron of Cerridwen and then you will travel into the depths of the Northern winter with Sedna, the Inuit Goddess of the Arctic Circle, so that you can experience the stillness, the void and space from which all is born.

In the Northern Hemisphere, the start of Samhain is in late October, mid autumn, and as the dark nights draw in there is still that feeling of getting everything ready for the winter, even though most of us now live in a world with twenty-four hour shopping and goods available to us from all seasons flown in from across the world. Our bodies instinctively tell us to be less active and as the colder months approach we can find it harder to wake up early and work the long days that are still demanded of us. You will utilise this time of the year to release those things in your life that are no longer working. You will perform ritual and meditation that allows you to release and work with your dreams. You will turn your attention inward, to incubate those things you wish to see grow in the future.

Working with the Seasonal Energies

Vivienne is Lady of the Lake. She is death and rebirth; she takes the souls of the dead to the afterlife or restoration across the mythic Lake of Avalon to the Isle of the dead. As Morgan the Priestess she is Arthur's sister and represents the Goddess, she takes the dying Arthur across the lake to Avalon to his resting place, where he does not die but instead waits to be reborn. Avalon is the otherworld and in the Glastonbury myth it is the Isle of Apples, which bear the fruit of the Goddess. If you cut an apple width ways, inside you will find a pentacle, the symbol of Venus and the Goddess. Avalon is the land of the Goddess and the Isle of the Dead, Inys Witrin, also known as the Glass Isle.

Vivienne is the aspect of the Crone Goddess who speaks to us in dreams and in myth; we lie still in the cauldron, waiting for our rebirth into the springtime, into the star fire. She is the source of all wisdom and we can journey with her as Priestess Shaman to the underworld where we can find those parts of our soul selves that need restoration. The cauldron represents her waters and she nourishes us through our journey into the afterlife.

Vivienne is often associated with 'the Fae ones' or the fairies; she is a magical creature who is described as 'arriving on the mist'. She is a shape shifter who can take water and change it to human form. In the Arthurian legend it is Vivienne who emerges from the lake of Avalon to present Arthur with his sword. This version of the story where she emerges from the lake associates her with the mermaid. She is a creature of the water; half woman, half fish. The crossing of water in Celtic mythology was analogous to death, the crossing over from one state of being to another. We find the Goddess in this place between life and death, her appearance from the lake heralding change and the transformation from one state to another. She is the deep wisdom of life, her gifts those of transformation and yet she is also death for she represents the ultimate change from one state to another. We work with her gifts of inner wisdom and she gives us the courage to face the inevitable change in our lives. The Lady of the Lake is the mysterious, the unknowable mystery of life, death and rebirth. She is ethereal, hard to pin down to one story and even her name shape shifts as she is variously known as Vivienne, Argante, Nimue and Niniane. In legend she is the foster mother of Lancelot, the consort and prisoner of Merlin; a prime mover in the Arthur stories initiating the characters and present at all the points of change. For she is the face of the ancient British Goddess, the primal force of life, omnipresent throughout all of its stages bringing deep wisdom and knowing. (*Ladies of the Lake,* Caitlin and John Matthews)

In ancient times, Avalon or Glastonbury was an island surrounded by an inland sea, so the lake of Avalon was actually an inland waterway reached by travelling along the River Brue. The marshy lands have been inhabited since Neolithic times and it is likely that the Celtic legends have much deeper roots back to the old Neolithic mother Goddess resonating with the water Goddesses of ancient times who were the primordial waters from which all life emerged.

As the wheel turns toward Yule, we meet with Sedna the

Inuit Goddess, she is the protectress of the whales, the seals and the sea creatures. She rages in anger and produces the sea storms of the winter as she remembers the deeds of her father when he threw her into the ocean out of his kayak, when he grew afraid of her husband who was searching for her. She is the dark angry side of the sea and the tumultuous stormy ocean; she is also wisdom, Goddess of the ancestors and grandmotherly love. Her frozen fingers became the whales and seals of the ocean and she is the protectress of the large sea mammals. She allows us to have the strength to leave behind those things in our lives that no longer serve our highest purpose.

Water holds the memories of all that has been and we will connect with Sedna to connect to our matriarchal line. She is the space and the void where we dream those things that we wish to manifest into our lives, as she lives at the bottom of the ocean in the depths and the dark. This is the only place on the planet that we cannot explore because of the pressure and it is a part of the Mother Earth of which we have little or no knowledge. From the nothingness all is created and we work with these Goddesses of Samhain and Yule to leave the past behind and to germinate the new.

The Transformative Practice of the Sea Priestess

The Wisdom of Water

Samhain and Yule (the winter) is the time of the crone; she is the grandmother, our matrilineal ancestor holding the wisdom of time and space. You will find her wisdom through the wisdom of water. The water that flows on the Earth now is the same water that has flowed on the Earth since the beginning of time. Locked away in the ice and snow are the memories of all that has been, all of life on Earth. That same water flows through us, connecting us to each other and to the Earth itself. Water as sentient life can communicate to us and inform us of all that has been if we take the time to connect and to listen.

Water illustrates the process of transformation, as dependent upon its temperature it takes different forms. In the autumn we find that as the temperature drops, moisture collects in the air producing fog and mist. As it descends the land becomes mysterious, shape shifting and producing shadow. In the Avalon tradition it is the mist that descends upon the lake that is then parted by the Priestess; it is she who can part the mists and enter the land of Avalon crossing the veil between the worlds.

In the winter it becomes ice and snow as the temperature drops below zero. We can see the strength in ice when we look back in time at the Earth's geology and see how glaciers have formed the land on which we live. These huge blocks of frozen water carved out valleys and deep canyons in the land, moving huge blocks of rock and stone miles on their icy current. We see the power of snow and ice when it brings the whole of Britain to a standstill during the winter months; but it can also bring out our playful side as we take snow days and play in this newly created winter wonderland. Each snowflake and ice crystal is individual with its own unique pattern and identity. These crystals are beauty in nature, perfectly formed and unique as we all are too. When we stand in the snow the air around us becomes dense and sound travels more slowly, giving that wonderful sense of peace and tranquility.

I remember as a child making snow crystals at school from paper and then hanging them around the classroom, each child's crystal was unique and yet individually they did not create the same impact as all of the designs hung together. Through these simple decorations we are able to remember our uniqueness and also our connection to each other and the deep wisdom that resides within us all.

And finally of course, as water increases in temperature it evaporates into the air, until eventually cooling and returning to Earth again to renew and begin its cycle. As Sea Priestess we will connect with this deep wisdom and remember our connection to all that has been and will be. We will deepen our connection to the water that is within us; that flows through our bodies, connecting us deeply to this blue planet.

The work of Dr Masaru Emoto showed that water reacts to emotion and to the thoughts that are projected upon it. Using high-speed photography he discovered that crystals formed in frozen water reacted differently dependant on the thoughts that were projected onto them. Water from clear springs spoken to in a loving way produced beautiful, complex and colourful snowflake patterns. Those that had been polluted and subjected to negative words and emotions were by contrast dull and incomplete. As our own bodies are 70% water then it would seem that the molecules contained within our body will function and perform better when they are also given love and where possible not subjected to toxic conditions.

Even though the earth is now moving into the cycle of winter it is important to spend time outside, to walk the land and feel the earth beneath your feet.

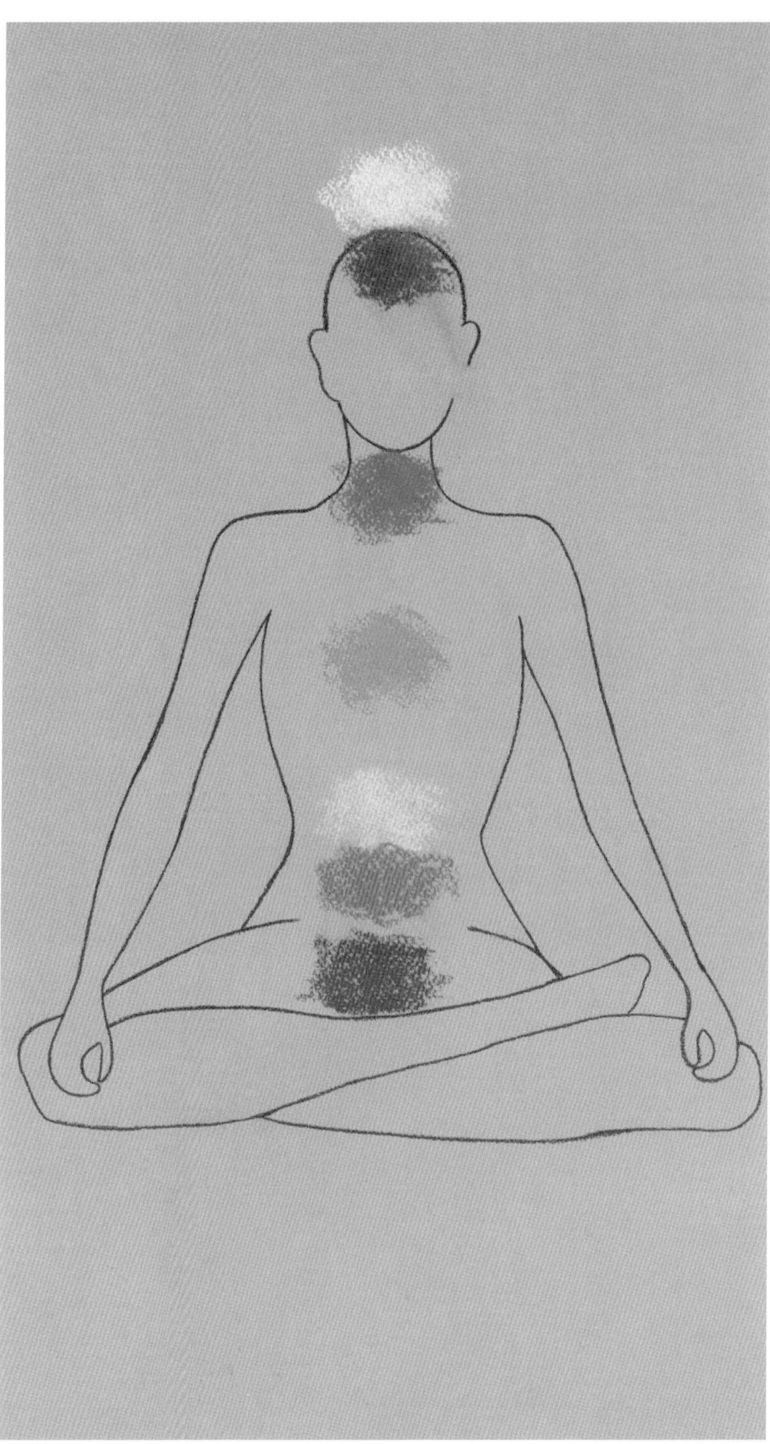

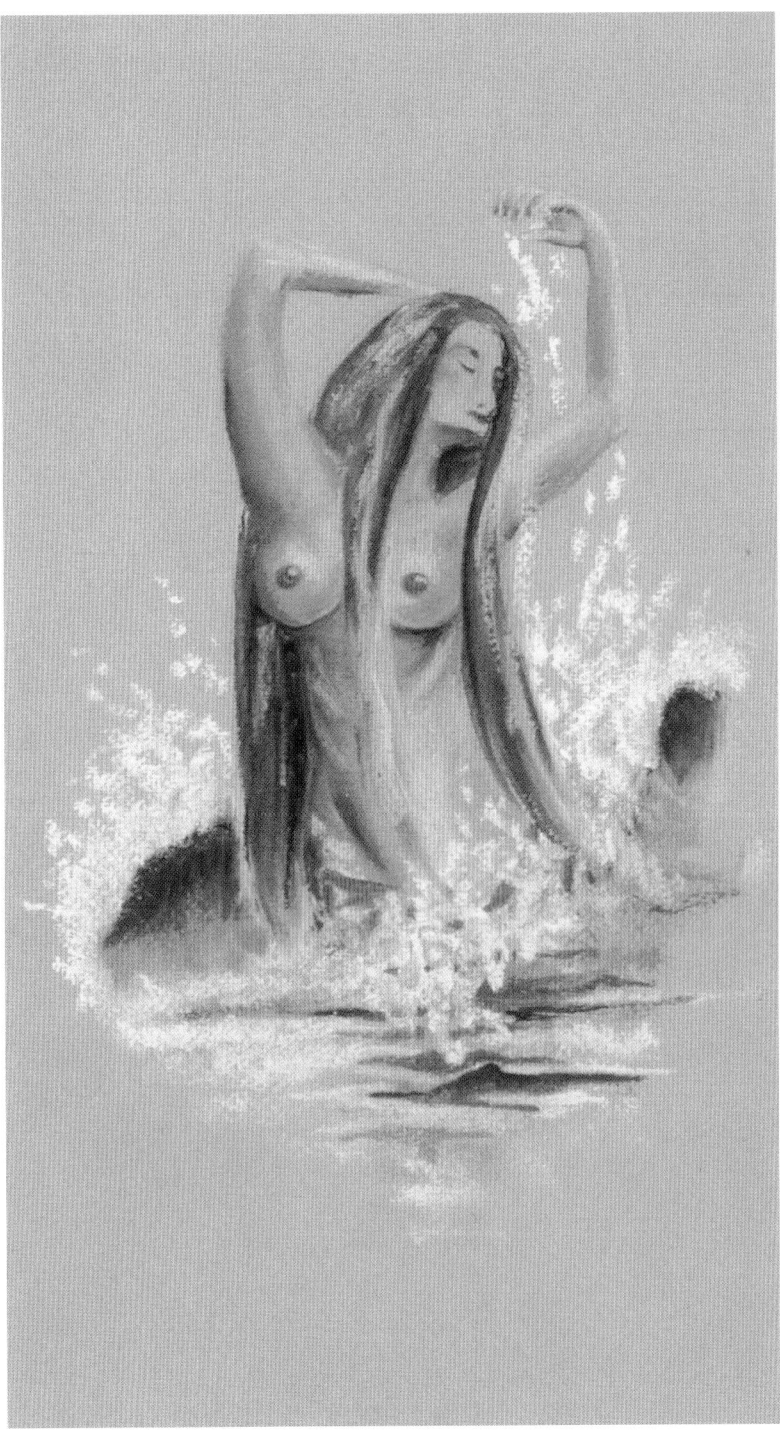

In the rest of this chapter you will find the exercises and meditations for the seasons of Samhain and Yule.

Grounding and Release

You can use the energies of Samhain to release those things in your life that are no longer helpful. Whether these are bad habits, unhealthy relationships or issues around self esteem, you can utilise the energies of the season to release these things and let them go, thereby making room in your life for those things you wish to encourage and see grow in the future.

You will work at Samhain with the lower chakra, that assists with elimination. The root chakra lies between the anus and the sex organs and is represented by a vortex opening down into the Earth. It is the chakra that grounds us and is responsible for elimination. Each chakra has a colour vibration associated with it and the root chakra is seen as red, the colour frequency with the lowest vibration. The Goddess aspect associated with the base chakra is courage and stillness.

The root chakra is associated with grounding and release. Whenever we feel that we are threatened or losing control in our lives it is the base chakra energy that is activated. However this can be inappropriate in our modern lives and we can find that the energies of this chakra become out of balance and we can express unresolved issues as inappropriate anger or aggression. If our self esteem is low then we can turn this inward and it's expression can be through negative behavioral traits such as addiction or negative thoughts and obsessive fears. Often where a person is trying to connect with higher energy and particularly when undertaking a spiritual path it becomes especially important to ensure that we remain grounded and that our base chakra is balanced. If we become ungrounded we can find that we are unable to properly release emotion and/or that we are unable to manifest our spiritual practice into our daily lives. An out of balance base chakra can manifest as fatigue and problems with the circulatory system. It is linked to the adrenal gland and is responsible for the flight or fight response. It is also linked to the lower skeletal structure of the hips, legs and feet. It is our flight or fight emotional response and it is closely identified to our sense of self. It is the energy centre closest to the Earth and therefore it connects us to the Earth itself. (*Crystal, Colour and Chakra Healing,* Sue and Simon Lilly)

In the introduction chapter we learnt a grounding exercise, which you can also use as supplementary to the exercises in this chapter. You can also use something called, mind-full meditation, to fully ground yourself in the present.

Mind-full Meditation

Mindfulness requires us to be in the present moment at all times. It can help us to feel rooted in our lives and to become more aware. It requires concentration on the breath and on the current action. A good way to introduce mindfulness into your life is through a walking meditation. This is similar to walking the land, however in this exercise you are mindful of yourself as well as the external environment.

When you undertake this meditative walk you are fully bringing yourself into the present. How often do you find that when out walking, you are not truly there, maybe you are talking to a friend or partner; listening to music, or your mind is full of disassociated thoughts. A mindful walk requires you to walk in nature, in silence. As you walk you experience each step, and you co-ordinate each step with your breath. As your feet touch the ground you feel each step on the land and the wonder of the nature that surrounds you. To walk mindfully is actually more difficult than it sounds as you will find that your mind wanders and you lose concentration. As this happens allow it but then focus back on the breath and each step. This very simple exercise is deeply grounding. You can also use the technique when you are undertaking any practical task. It's a great meditation for doing the washing up!

Ocean of Release

At Samhain we are entering a time of darkness and our thoughts become more inward looking. We are diving into who we are and dreaming of who we wish to become.

You will do this ritual at the dark moon, the night before the new moon is ideal.

Releasing Ceremony

You will be performing this ceremony to help release those things in your life that you believe aren't working anymore. In a releasing ceremony you are acknowledging to the universe and to Goddess that you are ready to release so that you can allow the new to enter. Change and transformation can only come where there is space for the new to enter. Goddess changes everything she touches and in undertaking this practice you are acknowledging that you wish your life to change in some way. You are remembering who you are and in doing so you need to release the old habits that do not serve this path and then welcome the new habits you wish to attain. Part of releasing is planting the new seed of the idea that you wish to see develop for the future. During this dark time of the year you will incubate the idea for its fruition in the coming spring.

You will perform this ceremony near water, either a fast flowing river or the sea is best. You will be putting your intention into a biodegradable object such as a stick, leaf, stone or something you believe represents your intentions. The item should be something from nature. If you can, go somewhere undisturbed so that you can perform the entire ceremony outside, if that's not possible then you can do the bulk of the ceremony at home and then travel to water for the final part.

A day or so before your ceremony go to the beach or park, take a long mindful walk and while you are doing so think of those things in your life that are no longer serving your best purpose. When I did this ceremony I desired to change where I was living as the house was in a very noisy area and no longer suited my lifestyle. As you walk look in nature for something that represents what you wish to release, this could be a shell or a stone for example. You may have more than one thing you wish to release and in which case it's fine to have more than one object. Don't have too many things though because this will confuse your intention. Sticking to one to three items is best. Remember you can do this exercise as many times as you need.

Take the object home and place on your home altar as a

representation of what you need to release. The reason for taking your time with this is to clarify whether it's a thing or an emotion you wish to release and whether what you are doing serves the highest good. For me I didn't really need to release the home (although this happened anyway over time) what I needed was to find some space and time in my life and to release the need to constantly be on the go 24/7. In this way I gained the peace I craved. Once you are happy with your intended release ask yourself what it is you would like to put in its place. In my case it was to give myself an hour each day where I was doing something for me rather than for other people.

On the day of your ceremony prepare a sacred space by placing objects representing the elements in their direction (using the wheel as directed earlier) or intuitively put the object in the direction you feel is right. In the centre place your chalice.

Start by grounding and centering yourself, stand with your feet firmly planted on the ground. Breathe deeply and imagine yourself rooted to the Earth. Feel the energies of the Earth coming up through your feet until they reach your heart. Then send your energies out and upwards to the heavens until you reach your mother star and then bring this star fire back to Earth, drawing it back down through your crown and into your heart. Let this heart energy fill you and expand outwards around you. When you feel centered in yourself you may then wish to ask the Goddess of Samhain to be present with you in the space. When speaking to the Goddess, do so in a respectful way, asking her if she wishes to be there with you. Ask for her qualities to be available to you for releasing the emotions or things you need to release. Once you have done this, take the object you found that represents this desire and pass it through each of the elements, stating your intention. So using my release as an example:

Air – *I ask that I have the wisdom to acknowledge my need for peace in my life and I release to air unwelcome noise.*

Fire – *I ask that I have the will to release my need to constantly please*

Water – *I ask that all noise and disruption flow out of my life and in its place I find stillness and contemplation*

Earth – *I ask that I release all that is not needed for my life's journey and I am in gratitude for peaceful and contemplative space.*

Finally, picking up your chalice, place the objects within the chalice and state your intention to release.

'Goddess I ask that for the highest good of all to release the noise and disruption in my life'

Then taking your chalice and your objects, one after the other ask the water to release them from your life and throw them into the water.

Thank the water and the Goddess of the season for their help in releasing.

Cerridwen' s Cauldron Meditation

Cerridwen is a Welsh Goddess or Lady of the Lake. She is an underworld Goddess of death and rebirth, growing with the waxing moon. She is the great white sow and keeper of the cauldron of transformation, which in the landscape of Snowdonia is Lake Tegid, a large bowl-like lake.

In her story, Cerridwen is a shape shifting Goddess, who brews a potion in her cauldron Amen, the intention being to gift her ugly son, Morfen (Sea Crow) or (Affadgu/Utter Darkness) with magical abilities. Her intentions are thwarted though, when Gwion the servant boy drinks three drops from his finger and becomes the gifted poet, Taliesin. A furious Cerridwen chases after the boy but as she does so he begins to shape shift into different creatures in his bid to escape the Goddess. First he is a hare and she changes into a greyhound, then a salmon with the Goddess becoming an otter. Lastly he becomes a grain of corn and Cerridwen a hen, where she promptly eats him. She then births him again as Taliesin the great poet and unable to harm him she tosses him into the ocean where he is found by Elphin and becomes a foster son of Gwyddno. This tale is from the Welsh legends of the Mabinogion and it is obvious that Cerridwen is a powerful ancient Goddess of death and rebirth; her cauldron is one of transforming energies that can help us to move from one state to another. This ancient Goddess births us, and then takes us back into her womb at death, ready to be reborn again. Working with this Goddess is deeply transformative and we can work with her at times of change in our life or when we wish to receive deep healing. She aids us with the process of change from one state to another, healing us while she allows us to rest with her through the dark nights.

This meditation is a journey into her cauldron to find healing and rest.

Finding somewhere peaceful where you will not be disturbed, sit or lie down and close your eyes. Take a number of deep breaths to relax yourself and then working from your feet upward, tighten each muscle and then relax. From your feet move to your calves, then your thighs, buttock muscles, back, arms, neck and face, tightening and then releasing as you move through each part of the body. Let yourself sink into the chair or floor. Imagine yourself floating in water, your body is weightless and you are able to float without any need to move your arms or legs. The water is warm, like the embryonic fluid in which we float in our mother's womb prior to birth. Allow yourself to be totally held here. You are in Cerridwen's cauldron, the place where you wait before your rebirth. Listen to your breath as you lie there totally supported. Know that you are always supported in all that you do, that you are held and loved. This is where you can come for peace, healing and renewal. Allow yourself to stay in this relaxed space for as long as you need. When you are ready to return, start wiggling your hands and feet, first one side then the other, stretch your arms and your legs, bring your knees to your chest and move from side to side. Allow yourself to come fully back into the present moment grounded and renewed.

The Dreaming

As we move towards Yule we enter the darkest part of the year. This is the time of the dreaming where we can truly enter our inner world. This time of the year is associated with the Goddess as Sedna the Inuit Goddess of the northern oceans. We will remember her and all that has been and in our re-memberance we will honour her. We utilise her energies to find our inner wisdom, the deep knowing that we all have within ourselves. In order to find what we seek we only need look to ourselves for within us are the answers that we seek. This is a time of meditation, of honouring the ancestral matriarchal line and of the dreaming.

'While I slept I dreamed. What I dreamed I do not remember,' (*The Sea Priestess,* Dion Fortune pg 87)

The aboriginal peoples of Australia believe that the universe was created during the dreamtime. They believe that each individual exists within the dreamtime as well as in their daily reality. When we are asleep we all dream during the REM cycle of sleep, generally for about two hours, for all of human existence we have been fascinated by what our dreams mean and the relevance of them to our daily existence. Pre-cognitive dreams where people believe they have seen the future have been widely documented, as have the interpretations of what dreams mean. Our ancestors believed that dreaming held special significance and Priestesses of old would dream for their peoples to see the future. In this work we pay special attention to our dreams as they can help us to more clearly understand what is going on in our lives and the changes and transformations we can and may need to make. Our dreams can often hold subconscious thoughts and fears that reveal themselves in the patterns of our dreams but that which we are unable to clearly understand in our conscious state.

In order to understand your dreams it is essential to keep a dream diary, during this period through Yule until the start of Imbolc you will keep a dream diary, alongside your moon diary observations. It doesn't matter if at first you can't remember your dreams clearly, just write down any thoughts and observations that come, even just what kind of night you had, i.e. deep sleep, restlessness. In your dream diary you are looking for patterns and recurrent themes. It's important that you write down your thoughts immediately upon waking as you will find that your dreams quickly fade as you move into the conscious state and your normal daily life. This doesn't have to take very long and the important thing is to keep your journal and a pen on your nightstand so that as soon as you wake you can record your dream. You will find that the act of recording your dreams on a daily basis will actually help you to recall your dreams and a dream journal can be an effective way to aid lucid dreaming.

Lucid Dreaming

Lucid dreaming is where we become conscious that we are dreaming and can influence our dreams. It is something that anyone can learn to do. By writing your dream diary you are already able to understand any recurrent themes or people that occur in your dreams and therefore you are more likely to understand when you are dreaming. You need to give yourself a trigger, something that lets you know whether you are awake or dreaming. You can do this by having a symbol that lets you know you are dreaming or by seeing if an object obeys the laws of gravity. A tried and tested method is to wake yourself up by setting your alarm clock for a few hours before you would normally wake, getting up and doing something and then after ten minutes or so going back to bed and visualising the lucid dream you wish to have. The benefits of lucid dreaming are that you are able to work consciously with your subconscious and thereby change your ingrained habits or leave behind those things that are no longer assisting you in your life. Lucid dreaming can also be used to act out those things you wish to see in your life and the conditions that you wish to create. By manifesting in your dreams you can go a long way toward manifesting your desires in your daily reality.

There are many good books and online resources that can be used to help you understand the content of your dreams, but, it is important that you also allow your intuition to help you to interpret your dream meanings. You can do this through meditation or just looking for patterns and themes. It can also help if you ask friends or relatives to tell you about their dreams and you can help them to interpret what those dreams mean for them. By exposing yourself regularly to dream like images you will be tuning into the subconscious world.

Water Memory

Water holds the memories of the planet and reveals the history of our climate and of our world. Water memory is the science behind homeopathic remedies, introducing the idea that water holds the memory of the substance introduced even when that substance is almost entirely removed from the water. As we are mostly water, we retain within us the memories from childhood and throughout our life within our very being and the water that comprises us. Generations of memory are stored within our DNA, we floated in the uterine waters of our mother before birth, so as well as our memories, memory of our matrilineal ancestors is also stored within us. At Yule we will honour our matrilineal ancestors and ourselves by blessing the water that is within us. We will do this through a self-blessing ceremony.

Self-blessing Ceremony

We all like a special bath-time and this ceremony is one that we can create for ourselves around bathing. Create a sacred space within your bathroom by lighting candles and burning sweet smelling incense. Invite the Goddess into the space. Bathe yourself and honour your body by blessing it with the water in which you are bathing. Imagine these wonderful blessings entering the water that is within you and surrounding you in your bath. Imagine your maternal ancestors going back for seven generations, their essence and memories also within this water. Imagine the blessings they would bestow on you, their darling granddaughter. Soak in these wonderful blessings, say them out loud, and feel them within the space. When you have finished your bath take some of the water and place in your chalice. When you have dressed take this water out and pour onto the land adding your blessings to the Earth and the water that flows upon it. This ceremony can also be performed in any body of water (weather permitting) and is fantastic when bathing in the sea.

Notes

Notes

8

Imbolc and Spring Equinox

The healing power of water is immense; emerging yourself into the sea, or into warm water, soothes the aches of the body as well as the aches of the mind. It is no wonder that the concept of the spa is seen as the ultimate indulgent luxury. At Imbolc and Spring Equinox we look to the healing powers of water, to heal and cleanse us. Here we work with the Goddesses of the wells and springs, the Goddesses of the rivers flowing as they do to the sea. Water has long been regarded as purifying and cleansing and, in the Christian tradition, as holy. It is no coincidence that the rite of baptism requires the subject to be immersed in water.

There are many benefits extolled in regards to the healing power of water, and throughout time people have either drunk or bathed in water to imbibe these healing properties. In the UK we can still see the clear evidence of healing water spas left by the Romans. The taking of the waters at places such as Bath in Somerset is believed to give healing and rejuvenation to all, and these spas have been restored and are still very much in use today.

Although the winter months are still with us, we can begin to see signs of new life emerging on the land and as the moon moves closer to the Earth at Spring Equinox and her magnetic powers increase, we experience the rise of the sea tides and increase in all of nature and in ourselves. At this time we will ask for healing of our emotions and we will use our chalice to perform healing and cleansing ceremonies and rituals. As the winter begins to recede and we move into spring, we will work with our natural creative source to further develop our projects and dreams.

In the past, springs were experienced as the openings into the Earth that led to the Goddess, and the waters that flowed from them were her life giving waters. In this practice we will celebrate the Goddess at the season of Imbolc as Coventina, the North East British Goddess of the springs and wells. Her most important site in Britain is at Carrawburgh, close to Hadrians wall near the border between England and Scotland; where there are shrines to her with offerings of coins and other (particularly) stone objects. Her name is of Celtic derivation and there is also evidence of her in North West Spain and in Gaul. Coventina is associated with healing, but she is also associated with renewal, abundance, new beginnings, inspiration and childbirth.

At Imbolc we will explore the healing power of water and the use of water to cleanse and purify, then as we move towards Spring Equinox we will give birth to our creative projects.

The Healing Waters of Imbolc

Imbolc is celebrated on or around the 2nd February. It is a cross quarter festival and it is associated with healing, fertility and with initiation. At the time of Imbolc we will heal ourselves and bring forth those things we have dreamt and nurtured throughout the winter months. It is a time of fecundity and of fertility. The nights are still long and the day's are cold but in the earth around us we can begin to see the first signs of this new fertility; the snowdrops emerging from the cold ground and the newly born lambs in the fields. We work with the Goddess at this time in her maiden aspect; she is the child full of wonder at the world, eager and celebratory. We will use this time to travel to her wells and springs and give thanks for our journey through the winter months. In times gone by, surviving winter was something to be grateful for and the arrival of even the early spring when the weather could still be bad was welcomed and celebrated by all.

At Imbolc we will also work to send healing to water, to the oceans that have become polluted. At the time of writing this book, the Japanese people are suffering from the power of water that has engulfed their land as a Tsunami. The power of which has damaged nuclear reactors causing radiation to spill into the water around their coasts. As terrible as this is, it is just one instance of where humans have polluted the coastal regions, oceans and seas. The sea has a great ability to heal and cleanse itself, yet we put more and more pollutants into the water and this natural system of cleansing is close to breaking down. The seas and oceans are the life force of this planet and in sending healing to the planet's waters, we help ourselves in the process.

Following is a meditation to send healing to the seas and water. As well as meditating though, we should also follow up with more practical action by becoming involved in charities and organisations that exist to help clean up our oceans. Undertake some personal research into how and where you would like to be active and then get out there and do it.

Meditation for Healing the Waters

As we have done in previous exercises, call the energies of the Goddess into the space then ground and centre yourself. Allow yourself to enter a meditative state by listening to your breath. If you are able try to do this meditation next to a body of water (preferably the sea) you will need to use your imagination less and will find that the meditation is more powerful. Allow your breath to flow in time with the tide as it laps in and out. Feel yourself becoming at one with the water. Feel any pollutants that are within the water and how this makes you feel, allow the Goddess's energy that you have called into the space to take these pollutants and neutralise them. Feel this energy flow back and forth between yourself and the ocean, removing and neutralising those elements that as humans we have placed within the waters to cause this pollution. Know that whilst you undertake this exercise, that Goddess is flowing around and within you, protecting you from any harmful impact. For at the same time as she is cleansing the pollutants from the ocean, she is cleansing the waters that flow within you and restoring you too, to perfect health. When you feel ready say a prayer of thanks to the sea for its life sustaining properties and to the Goddess for her cleansing and love.

This meditation is a great way of attuning yourself with the sea whilst at the same time working to heal the waters. As we have seen from previous chapters, water is remarkable in that it holds memory, the water will hold the memory of this cleansing you have assisted with. In doing so you are restoring yourself and the water back to its natural and pure state.

Fertility

Imbolc is a time of fertility where the earth is quickened and prepared. We will utilise this time to fertilise the projects we have dreamt about during Samhain and Yule. The most famous quote from Dion Fortune's The Sea Priestess is:

'Learn now the mystery of the ebbing and flowing tides. That which is dynamic in the outer is latent in the inner.' (*The Sea Priestess,* Dion Fortune pg 163)

In this statement Fortune was trying to explain that there is the internal world of dreams, imagination and emotion and then the external world of practicality, action and creation. We can associate this too with the elements, where air and water rule thought and emotion. Ideas and feelings are internalised and do not yet exist as form and then earth and fire where these thoughts and feelings become grounded in reality and come into existence. In undertaking this practice we are working with the dream world and with the emotions, however in order for those to take form they need to move through fire and earth in order to become potent in the outer world. Fortune's Sea Priestess used a partner, Wilfred, in her acts of magic and working together they gave form to her dreams. In this practice we are daring to be both potent in the inner and outer worlds so that we can bring our dreams to manifestation.

As you move with the wheel of the year you are moving your dreams into reality so that you can experience them in the world of form, as well as in meditation and your dreams. You will use your chalice to perform a ceremony of fertilisation and take your dreams and spark them with life.

Looking back to the work that you did in the moon meditations, think about those dreams you wished to bring into manifestation. Take another look at your vision board and dream diary to bring these clearly into focus.

Using your chalice you are going to perform a ceremony of fertilisation. This ceremony can also be used if you are wishing to actually become pregnant.

To perform this ceremony you will need to prepare the following:

• Your altar set up with the four directional elements and any images, statues you wish to place on it.
• An item to represent the elements, a candle for fire; incense for air, water and perfume/rose oil for earth.
• Your chalice
• A candle that can float in water
• Purifying incense such as white sage
• Spring water enriched with iron (look for a brand which has high iron content)

Beginning the ceremony, ground and centre yourself and then call the energy of the Goddess into the space. Then, moving around your altar, pass through each element. So, for example as you pass through air, smudge yourself by taking a feather and wafting the incense over and through your body and your auric field. This is a very honouring thing to do to another person and this ceremony works very well for a group to perform together. Then, moving to fire, pass the flame across your body making sure not to burn yourself, then splash yourself with water and finally for earth, anoint yourself with perfume or oil. Rose oil is very good for this purpose.

Then, taking your chalice, fill it with the spring water enriched with iron. Then thinking about those things you wish to bring into form, transfer those thoughts into the water by passing the white sage incense stick across the chalice, imbuing the water with the incense smoke, imagine your dreams entering this realm of water, entering the womb space of your chalice. Then finally take the floating candle and light it from the candle on your altar and vision your dreams being fertilised by the fire. Allow the candle to burn out floating in the water. Thank the Goddess for being with you in the space.

The most important part of the ceremony is now to start actively working on your dreams in your daily life. So for example if you have a project that you wish to start, begin work on it. Start the preparatory work by talking to the right people, putting plans down on paper etc. This is very important and shows the universe that you are serious in bringing your intention into form. Also, if you are actually wishing to become pregnant, this means engaging in regular sexual activity with your partner and pursuing fertility issues with your doctor if you are experiencing difficulties in becoming pregnant. This is the true meaning of being potent in the outer as well as in the inner, in that we must walk in both realms.

Spring Equinox

Spring Equinox is one of my most favourite times of the year. The Earth is literally springing back into life and the days become longer and warmer and my energy levels naturally increase. As I spend time near the sea, the spring tides emulate the fullness that is starting to be experienced on the land. The sea seems to move to join with the land becoming one.

As we move into the greening time, where all is new and the land comes back to life after the winter, we work with the Goddess as Sabrina, who is the river Severn that flows out into the Bristol Channel and creates the sea between Avon and South Wales. She is also known as Afron or Havron, and like the Nile the River Severn in the UK is a river that floods the land, bringing fertility. It has an unusual tidal surge known as the Severn Bore, which is an amazing and unique tidal flow caused by the shape of the river and the way that it funnels out to the sea. The tidal range of this river can be as much as fifty feet and in ancient times it would have brought fertility to the land that surrounded it as its tides ebbed and flowed with the seasons. We will work with Sabrina at this time of balance and of the Spring Equinox. The tides are high and the veil between the worlds is thin and we will use this time to practice the art of divination.

Divination

Divination is the art of looking into the future in order to help us understand our path by activating the precognitive abilities that we all have. It is not about superstition but about opening ourselves to the unseen world and working with it in order to understand our capabilities and our intuition. When working with our intuitive natures, we have a better understanding of ourselves and others and we can use imagery such as the tarot deck to help us move into this world, understanding our subconscious motivations. If we believe that our intention is what sets our future then it is only a small step to look into our subconscious to see what kind of future we are creating for ourselves. Our thoughts and words of now are creating our future and we have a responsibility to create the best future we can for ourselves. In doing so we have to remove the thought that life is somehow fated and that we cannot escape our destiny. For it is us that are creating our destiny, therefore it is us who are ultimately in control, in respect of the destiny our minds create.

People are often scared of divination, believing that somehow it is wrong to know the future and that they must just accept what 'fate' gives them. But in believing this they are limiting their lives and ultimately not living their lives to their fullest potential. There is no good or bad future as there is no judgment of the future, for with just one change of thought or word, so the future can be changed. The future is the same as now and the Sea Priestesses of old understood that. They were a channel and they did not ascribe emotional judgments to their knowledge, they knew that ultimately we all carry personal responsibility for our actions and that the result was of our own making. This can seem harsh for those people who experience quite upsetting lives and as a concept can be hard to grasp when bad things happen to seemingly good people, particularly if they are small children or vulnerable adults. Yet in believing we choose our own destiny and path, and that we choose our lives and how they should be lived, does not mean that we cannot help or reach out to those who are vulnerable in our society. In doing so, maybe that person chose their life to give you the gift of compassion. (*Positive Magic,* Marion Weinstein) There are many traditional methods of divination, tarot cards being the best known. But for the Sea Priestess practice we will divine through nature and through water. The art of divining through water is known as hydromancy. Our deep connection with water and the fact that our bodies are 70% water means that we can use this deep connection to assist with our divination techniques. People have divined using water for thousands of centuries, either by looking into wells, pools and fountains or using the sea. A simple method of divination is the childhood game of 'poo sticks', where two sticks are tossed into a river from one side of a bridge and the stick that comes out first wins. This form of divination can be used for a quick yes or no answer to a problem. The scrying mirror used by many pagans is just a more modern method of water divination, where the individual gazes into a pool and watches the images that appear in the still water as is done now with the mirror.

When divining using water, it's important to let your intuition lead you and even if your imagination brings out strange or unexplainable images, take note of them. It's a good idea to have a pen and paper handy when divining so that you can write down what you see. What may not make sense immediately may become much clearer over time, as dreams often do. Don't allow your preconceptions to determine what you see. Yes there will be some symbols that may have pre-ascribed meanings but try not to interpret too literally. Divination is a tool for opening your sub-conscious and intuition, so let your imagination be your guide.

The ideal time to divine using water is at the full moon when the connection between the water and the moon is at its greatest. If you do so whilst outside then all the better, as you will be able to see into the water by the light of the moon which will cast shadows and shapes into the water. Before divining you should allow yourself to become really relaxed, you can do this through the breath or by tensing and relaxing your body. Ground and centre and call the Goddess energy into the space. By now, the act of doing this will remind you that you are entering non-ordinary space. Then, looking into a bowl filled with water lit by the moon, allow your gaze to relax as if you are looking slightly beyond what you, are looking into. As you relax the muscles in your face and eyes take note of the images that appear in the water. When you have finished write down what you have seen. It may be just jumbled images or you may have seen clear images, whatever write them down without judgment. If you have seen nothing then again don't be concerned, it may be that you were not relaxed enough or that you are tired. Again release any judgment that you may have about yourself or your ability to divine. With practice this will become much easier and you will become skilled at knowing what the images mean to you.

Other methods of divining using water are to throw pebbles into the sea and see the patterns that form, or to use steam onto a mirror. You will also find your own methods over time. It is important to practice divination on a regular basis and you will find that your intuitive abilities increase as a result.

Notes

Notes

January

1	2	3	4
5	6	7	8
9	10	11	12
13	14	15	16
17	18	19	20
21	22	23	24
25	26	27	28
29	30	31	

February

1	2	3	4
5	6	7	8
9	10	11	12
13	14	15	16
17	18	19	20
21	22	23	24
25	26	27	28
29			

March

1	2	3	4
5	6	7	8
9	10	11	12
13	14	15	16
17	18	19	20
21	22	23	24
25	26	27	28
29	30	31	

April

1	2	3	4
5	6	7	8
9	10	11	12
13	14	15	16
17	18	19	20
21	22	23	24
25	26	27	28
29	30		

May

1	2	3	4
5	6	7	8
9	10	11	12
13	14	15	16
17	18	19	20
21	22	23	24
25	26	27	28
29	30	31	

June

1	2	3	4
5	6	7	8
9	10	11	12
13	14	15	16
17	18	19	20
21	22	23	24
25	26	27	28
29	30		

July

1	2	3	4
5	6	7	8
9	10	11	12
13	14	15	16
17	18	19	20
21	22	23	24
25	26	27	28
29	30	31	

August

1	2	3	4
5	6	7	8
9	10	11	12
13	14	15	16
17	18	19	20
21	22	23	24
25	26	27	28
29	30	31	

September

1	2	3	4
5	6	7	8
9	10	11	12
13	14	15	16
17	18	19	20
21	22	23	24
25	26	27	28
29	30		

October

1	2	3	4
5	6	7	8
9	10	11	12
13	14	15	16
17	18	19	20
21	22	23	24
25	26	27	28
29	30	31	

November

1	2	3	4
5	6	7	8
9	10	11	12
13	14	15	16
17	18	19	20
21	22	23	24
25	26	27	28
29	30		

December

1	2	3	4
5	6	7	8
9	10	11	12
13	14	15	16
17	18	19	20
21	22	23	24
25	26	27	28
29	30	31	

9

Beltane and Summer Solstice

And so we turn to the subject of love. This is the life affirming way of the Sea Priestess. At this time we will learn to love ourselves, for in doing so we will learn the power of love so that we may open our hearts and feel love and compassion for all. In this chapter you will open your heart and allow love to flow through your heart chakra, radiating out to the world around you. At Beltane you will work with the lover Goddess Aphrodite as the awakener of love and as Nimue of the waterfall, beloved of Merlin. Then as we move toward the Summer Solstice you will bathe with Sulis Goddess of the hot springs and Domnu, great mother of the oceans.

One of the most powerful and magical energies within this dimension is the power of love. It has the ability to transform all that is. Looking through the eyes of love we see each other in a new way, we can see past outer appearance to the soul beneath. Love can cause us to do amazing things. The love of the mother for her child can cause her to sacrifice her own life in place of theirs. Love can also be destructive when it is unrequited or out of balance, causing jealousy, hurt and emotional upset. Love is compassion, seeing potential in our-self and others. Love can be blind to faults and misdemeanors. Love can take us to new places within ourselves and spur us on to achieve great things. It is no surprise that the subject of love is one that is written about, sung about, displayed in works of art in whatever culture we live in or whatever language is spoken. Love takes many forms, from the union of lovers, to the love that exists between family members and then to the love that can be shown for all of the Earth and the people and nature that exist upon it. Finally there is spiritual love that transcends all and is the fuel of magic.

In Dion Fortunes' book, through the story of Morgan and Wilfred we discover a story of love, a bond created by spiritual work, not consummated through sexual fulfillment but through the polarity of male and female working together to be all women and all men through the alchemy of love.

'All the Goddesses are one goddess and we call her Isis, the all woman, in whose nature all natural things are found; virgin and desirous by turn, giver of life and bringer in of death. She is the cause of creation, for she awakeneth the desire of the All Father.' (*The Sea Priestess,* Dion Fortune pg 217)

For love is magic, it is pure alchemy that can change the inner and the outer world. When we fall in love it creates a chemical reaction in the brain, our pupils dilate, we become flushed and the blood rises to the skin and to the sexual organs, preparing us for the bliss of union with another soul. In tantric tradition this union raises energy and allows for connection with the divine in our-self and the divine in another. Love is a magic that changes all who come into contact with it. In this chapter we will explore love in all its aspects and bring this energy into our lives so that we may surrender to the bliss that it can bring.

Aphrodite the awakener

'Golden Aphrodite cometh not as the virgin, the victim, but as the 'awakener, the desirous one' (*The Sea Priestess,* Dion Fortune pg 216)

The element of water is a passive element rather than an active one. Yet in Aphrodite we find a Goddess associated with the element of water; who is also the awakener, active and bringing forth the power of love through her beauty. Aphrodite is one of the Greek goddesses of Olympus. She is the white foam of the waves brought forth when Cronus mutilated his father, Uranus, by severing his genitals and throwing them into the sea. She is a love Goddess with three aspects; Aphrodite Urania includes the ideal or pure love, Aphrodite Genetrix who is the patroness of married couples and finally Aphrodite Pandemos who is the Goddess of lovers, mistresses and courtesans. Aphrodite's birth from the sea is a reflection of the close connection between water and physical love, sexuality and fertility.

It is in her aspect as Genetrix (Genesis) that we see the awakening power of Aphrodite for it is her passion that is planted into the human soul and which awakens the desire that lives within it. She is a fertility Goddess who uses the power of love to bring forth all of creation. Aphrodite is often portrayed emerging from the ocean on a seashell or surrounded by water nymphs. However in Aphrodite's many stories the awakening of love can be a painful and transformational experience. In the tale of Aphrodite and Adonis, who she takes as a mortal lover, his death sees him taken to the underworld to reside with

Persephone. Aphrodite mourns his passing, her tears becoming the anemone flower and she begs Persephone to allow Adonis to reside with her for six months of the year, and so Adonis becomes another symbol of nature blooming and withering away each year, a symbol of the power of nature over which Aphrodite is the protectress.

It is as the awakener of love that we will work with Aphrodite at Beltane, in modern times she has often been associated with the mirror. Aphrodite's mirror is a metaphor for being able to see oneself with love. For as the bringer of love, if Aphrodite looked at herself in a mirror then all she would see would be love, for she is love. How we look and how we see ourselves in the modern world is a subject that warrants reams of coverage from women's magazines, to newspapers, television and cinema. We are constantly bombarded from a young age with representations of what the perfect woman should look like and how society believes a woman should look. If we differ from this norm, which is not really a norm at all (as 99.9% of the population do not conform) then we can believe incorrectly that we are not beautiful and more painfully that we are therefore inherently un-loveable. Unfortunately for countless women their self-image is poor and they believe that if they could only change part of the way they looked, that they would be happier, more successful and more likely to find love. *(Glamour magazine,* Shaun Dreisbach 2011) surveyed 16,000 of their readers and found that 97% had negative thoughts about their body image daily. These brutal thoughts about their body image included 'you're a fat worthless pig', 'gross', 'your too thin', 'no man is ever going to want you' to name just a few. These thoughts were not from outsiders but from the women themselves who berated their own body image and who thought these things about themselves on a daily basis. To fully open ourselves to love we have to love ourselves first. Your own thoughts may be not as cruel or as frequent as the *Glamour* readers but I would question any woman who had not looked in the mirror and criticized some part of herself and I would also congratulate her for she has been able to transcend the negativity surrounding the media and society's obsession with the looks of women beyond any other quality she may possess.

Aphrodite Mirror Exercise

We will perform this mirror exercise to awaken love for the self and to teach ourselves to love our own bodies and the soul within. This exercise can be a difficult one for many women and it's not unusual for some women to have not looked at certain parts of their body their entire adult life. This exercise begins with looking at your face only. Before you begin remove any make-up you are wearing and pin your hair back so that you can see all of your face.

As with all the other exercises we do in this book, call the Goddess energy into the space and take time to relax; breathing deeply and bringing you into a sacred space. Have next to you a hand mirror, when you are ready start to look into the mirror. Take in all your face, if you have any negative thoughts allow them but let them pass. They are not necessary for this exercise. Look at the bone structure below your skin, marvel at how your body is made; the skin, your eyes, nose and mouth. Take time to look at each part of your face acknowledging how complex it is, how much is going on. Look into your eyes and be amazed at how they give you a window on the world. See each part of your face as a piece of intricate machinery designed to do a job. How amazing that we have been created with such abilities. [Note if you are sight impaired, you can do this exercise through the power of touch, so substitute the mirror for you fingers and allow them to touch and feel the marvel of your face.] As you look at your face, look at how the face ages, how the marks on your face have changed from when you were younger. Be thankful for these laughter lines, these wrinkles and marks on the skin, which map your journey through life. See the wisdom that has been earned and the joy, pain, and love that you have witnessed. Then as you continue to look at your face give thanks for the gifts of sight, smell, taste and hearing that your face has given you. Then closing your eyes and putting the mirror to one side, imagine the Goddess Aphrodite's face and as you do so go through the same exercise as above, look at her bone structure, her skin, eyes, etc and see them as functioning parts of her body. When you have done this open your eyes and taking the mirror look, into it again. Note how you have exactly the same qualities as she does, and how beautiful and wonderful you are. Say a prayer of thanks to Aphrodite for her mirror.

As you move through the season of Beltane, take the opportunity to do this exercise on a regular basis. At first just look at parts of your body exclusively, as you have done with your face. Maybe start with your legs, your breasts or your arms. Eventually build the exercise until you are looking at your entire body. As with the earlier part of the exercise if you find yourself thinking negatively allow the thought but take no heed of it. Continue to see your body for the marvellous thing that it is, free from thoughts of how it should or could look. This exercise is designed to allow you to look at yourself free of judgment and dispassionately. Once you feel able to this then you are ready to begin looking at yourself with love and compassion.

This is where the second stage of the exercise begins. As above, bring yourself into a sacred space and relax by breathing deeply. Standing naked in front of a full-length mirror look at yourself; if you have done the exercises above you should now be able to look at yourself without judgment. Allow your eyes to flow across your body. Look at all the parts of your body. Look at those parts of your body you like and feel a deep appreciation for them. Then look at those parts you like less and feel the same level of appreciation. Then, continuing to look at yourself, perform the grounding and centering exercise, sending your energy down into the ground below you, down through your legs into the ground below, joining your energy with that of Mother Earth, then take that energy into your heart centre and allow it to flow out of your crown until it reaches your mother star and then bring that energy back down into your heart chakra. As you do so, see this heart energy filling your entire body and let this loving energy encompass your whole body. You are Aphrodite bathed in this wonderful heart chakra loving energy. See yourself in all your beauty and feel this love enter every cell of your body. You are Goddess and you are beautiful. Do this exercise as many times as you like and each time feel the love and appreciation for yourself and your body expand.

This exercise is an important one in the journey of the Sea Priestess, for in the ability to accept ourselves with all of our imperfections we can better tolerate the faults of others and we are less likely to feel threatened. Improving our relationships with others and our self esteem. Increased self worth means that we can build lasting and strong relationships with others. My lasting appreciation also to *Jane Meredith* who taught me the concepts of these exercises in a wonderful workshop I attended.

The Union of Lovers

Nimue is the lover of Merlin in the Arthurian legends, she is the grail maiden and the container of the feminine, the source of life. She is depicted by the waterfall and is known as an enchantress. She is known as the imprisoner of Merlin, capturing him so that his body perished but his spirit lingers on. He desires her and it is because of his constant sexual advances that he becomes imprisoned. She has become known as a sexual enchantress and yet at the same time she is also reminiscent of the virgin huntress. She desires the knowledge of Merlin and in return he wants sexual favour from her. Yet she uses his own desires against him in that once she has learnt his magic, she uses it to imprison him. Like a lot of the virgin Goddesses she is complete within herself and yet in Nimue we see the challenge that women experience when they leave childhood and become a woman. She has her own desires but must deal with the desires of others who wish to manipulate her to their own ends. In yet another version of the story Nimue is presented as a fey creature whose advances are spurned by Merlin and for this she destroys him. *(Ladies of the Lake, Caitlin and John Matthews)*

The experience of love is characterized by the flow of emotions between our-self and the object of our love. It can be a wonderful but scary experience where we open ourselves to another, showing our vulnerabilities, and this love can be rejected. Yet we need to understand this ebb and flow of emotion to truly allow and to accept love whilst at the same time understanding that this love can be lost. Trying to hold onto love is like trying to hold onto water flowing through the hands. If we try to do so then we can find that our sacral chakra causes an intense emotional response in our bodies and that our heart chakra becomes out of balance. This can lead to ill health and obsessive behavior. An unbalanced sacral or heart chakra can mean that we view the world from a childlike perspective where we are unable to place ourselves in the worldview of another.

As we mature and strengthen the heart chakra we become aware of the reality of our situation in that we can only live our own life and not the lives of others. Each one of us has our unique perspective and we need to understand and value the perspectives of others. We must follow our own path in life whilst allowing those we love to do the same. In this way we open our hearts to a more spiritual and compassionate understanding of others.

Wilfred also has to learn this lesson from Morgan, who he can love but can never own or truly call his. He can be with her for the time they have and then she will disappear from his life and all that he can call his own is the remembrance of that time. As she says to him in her last letter:

'Myself I could not give to you for it was not in my power' (*The Sea Priestess,* Dion Fortune pg172)

For no one has the power to be another or to live the life

of another, and this is a lesson that only love can teach.

Heart Chakra Exercise

In this exercise we will work with the heart chakra to bring balance to our relationship with others and to foster a compassionate understanding within ourselves.

To do this exercise we will use crystals. You will need to find or buy four green crystals. Aventurine or tourmaline in a green colouring is a good choice. You will also need one clear quartz crystal. Then you need to lie on the floor. Allow yourself to sink into the floor. Let your body fully relax and breathe into any areas that feel stiff or achy. Practice the deep breathing that you have learnt in the other exercises until your body feels totally relaxed. Then place the crystals in the following shape over your heart chakra, with the quartz crystal directly over your sternum and the green crystal slightly overlapping.

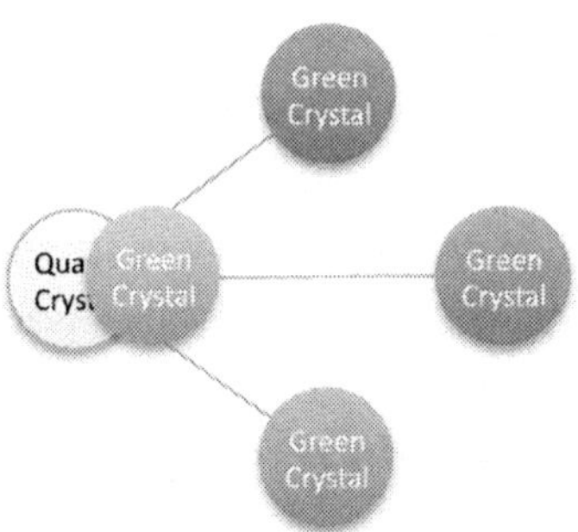

As you lie with the crystals placed in this configuration, imagine the green energy of your heart chakra radiating out across your body, bringing all of the cells of your body into balance and alignment. Allow the healing energy to flow and when you feel that it is complete, remove the stones from your chest start to wiggle your toes and your fingers bring your knees to your chest, and wriggle your spine left to right. Come back to a seated position and allow yourself a couple of minutes to come fully back into the room. (*Crystal, Colour and Chakra Healing,* Sue and Simon Lilly)

Poetry the Food of Love

The expression of love is often seen through art and the art of poetry allows us to express what we feel in our hearts in a unique way. Everyone is able to write poetry all though many people believe is it not possible for them. The thought of sitting with a blank piece of paper or of rhyming words can be very intimidating. Yet to express your thoughts onto paper can be a marvellous way of releasing inner emotion and expressing your deepest desires. The Sea Priestess understands that in allowing thoughts and desires, but not being controlled by them, that the natural flow of love can be enhanced. This next exercise is in the art of poetry writing and you are going to be writing a poem about love. This is a sacred poem that you can choose to keep after the experience or destroy. The poem is yours and does not need to be read or experienced by anyone else. As with the other exercises you should prepare a sacred space for writing your poem and do the grounding and centering exercise before beginning.

You are going to be writing your poem through a technique known as automatic writing, i.e. you are just going to write, do not read back what you have written and try and write for at least two minutes. Just allow the words to flow even if what you are writing is nonsense.

When you have done this, read back what you have written on your paper to yourself. See if a few key words stand out for you. Intuitively pick out those few words from the paper and write them on a new piece of paper. They will form the backbone of your poem. Taking those words spend five minutes writing about your feelings associated with them. Again you are just free writing. When you have finished, this time take the key sentences or words you have written.

You are now ready to write your poem. Take a further ten minutes to write your poem. Read it back to yourself and then you can either keep or destroy. Write in your journal how this experience was for you. You can do this exercise as many times as you like and over time you will find that your freedom of self expression will increase and that you will access your deeper subconscious needs and desires.

Summer Solstice

The longest day of the year and the sun is at its height. This is the time of year when we take our holidays and when we can enjoy the heat of the sun. Here we find the love of the Goddess as compassionate wisdom; she is the nurturing love, the chalice that contains the waters of life. She is the sacral womb energy that holds the gift of life. The image of the chalice as the womb space and the container is the gift of the Goddess. We will activate the sacral chakra and receive the blessings and pleasures of the Goddess.

Sacral Chakra Exercise

Detoxification is one of the purposes of the sacral chakra, it is closely associated with the element of water and it allows for the natural flow within our body. The sacral chakra is the second chakra from the base chakra and is situated in the womb space of a woman. This is the place where life is created and it is a creative powerhouse once awakened. When over stimulated it can lead to extreme emotional response but when closed it can cause blockages throughout the system and lessen our life force.

This exercise brings the sacral chakra into balance and stimulates the creative nature that is dormant within us all. One of the most opening exercises for the sacral chakra is belly dancing and the exercise that we will undertake is a similar movement.

Standing with your feet slightly apart take a number of deep breaths so that you feel relaxed and grounded. Then begin to breathe into the sacral chakra. Take a breath deeply into your lungs and feel it entering your womb space. Let each breath go deeper, feel it moving down into your lower abdomen. Move in the space with the effort of the breath. As you breathe begin to move your lower hips. Feel the breath enter the space and on the out breath move your hips in a circular motion. With each in breath move the hips in a clockwise motion and on the out breath move them in an anti-clockwise direction. Feel the womb space opening as you breathe and swing your hips. Do this for as long as feels comfortable. When you are ready come into a seated position on the floor. Sit as if you are going to cross your legs but instead bring your feet together, soles facing one another, and allow your knees to fall outwards. Make sure your back is straight. Sit like this for one or two minutes concentrating on the sacral womb space, and feeling the energy you created dissipate and return to the earth. If it is not possible for you to sit in this way sit on a chair with your legs spread apart and your feet touching.

Joy

Happiness and enjoyment are essential to our wellbeing and it is at this time of the year we take holidays and bathe in the warmer waters of the ocean. It is here we can work with Sulis. She is the ancient British Goddess of the hot springs of Bath, situated in the West Country of Britain. She is a life giving, nourishing Goddess where devotees would leave offerings at her hot springs. There is still a spa at Bath and if you have the opportunity you should visit. If not take the chance to visit a spa near you and luxuriate in the warm waters.

The process of bathing will allow for all of the stresses and strains of modern life to be washed away and it can bring a feeling of joy. Below you will find a meditation to meet with Domnu great mother of the Oceans, so even if you cannot get away for a summer break you can meditate on the pleasures of this experience.

Meditation to Journey with Domnu to the Waters of Life

Water provides us with nourishment and is required for all life on Earth. The Earth is the blue planet because of the water that flows over it. We cannot live longer than three to five days without water. It sustains us and provides us with our life force. Water is life itself and we will journey to Domnu, Goddess of the waters who is the nurturing and life giving Goddess.

Lie down or sit somewhere where you are comfortable.

Make sure that you won't be disturbed and keep yourself warm and concentrate on your breathing. Listen to the rhythm of your breathing; follow the breath in and out. Allow your body to relax. Let go of all of your external thoughts, allow them but let them pass.

Imagine in your mind's eye that you are seated on a beach, you can feel the sand beneath your bare feet and a light breeze touches your bare shoulders. You can hear the sand moving as the tide moves in and out, the waters almost reach your feet. The sun is shining in the blue sky above you and only a small occasional cloud comes into view. You are feeling very rested and peaceful as you sit here on this beautiful beach. Allow yourself to just sit and be for a moment, the sun warming and healing your body, the sand gently massaging your feet whilst the cooling breeze keeps you comfortable. You look out into the waters and watch as the tide moves in and out; it's movement echoing your breath. Breathe with the tide for a while.

You begin to notice small reflections on the water, tiny ripples and bubbles, and you stand up and enter the sea to discover what is causing them. The water flows gently around you're ankles as you step in, the cooling water on your feet. You wade into the water following these small ripples that are moving further out to sea. You soon find that you are waist deep and you take the opportunity to lower yourself into the water to swim, the coolness of the water making you gasp slightly as it covers your shoulders. As you swim though it begins to feel warmer and you enjoy the sensation of being supported by the salty water, allowing yourself to lie on your back, gently floating with only the smallest movement of your feet required to keep you afloat.

As you lie in the water you notice a fin and then the head of a dolphin appearing above the water right next to where you are floating. It moves toward you and you place your hand on its head, feeling the warmth of its skin. It invites you to hold onto its fin and you swim together. The dolphin telepathically asks you if you want to see what lies under the water. If you want to dive with it then allow yourself to be taken under the water. The dolphin is your guide and is leading you further down into the water. You discover to your surprise that you have no trouble breathing under the water and you feel very comfortable as you descend. As you travel further with the dolphin you see a pod of them and they perform an underwater display for you; their grace and poise is beautiful as they circle each other before rising above the waves. You look further down and see a school of tuna fish, like a huge mass they move as if one, below them are rocks and schools of tinier fish.

Deeper and deeper you swim until the light from above has disappeared and all around you is blackness. Strange creatures with reflective lights pulse around you providing the only light in the impenetrable darkness. Blacker than the night sky for no stars light this world and the glow from the creatures pulsates and reveals their presence rather than penetrating the blackness.

You continue to swim down into an abyss, down into to the depths of the ocean for it is here where Domnu and her children dwell, here in the primordial darkness of the deep ocean. As you swim into the nothingness, into the blackness notice how you feel.

Finally you see a glimmer of light and you swim toward it,

faster now as the undersea current sweeps you onward. Then all is light and around you is Domnu's Queendom a place of beautiful halls of rock and fluorescent light. One of Domnu's children swims towards you and the dolphin bids you goodbye as it swims back to the surface. This is your guide, speak with them for a while and get to know them. They then ask you:

'Are you ready to meet with Domnu Queen of the Oceans?'

You must choose now. Will you meet with Domnu?

If your choice is yes then go with them to her.

Leaving you alone now, you are in the company of the Goddess Domnu. Imagine how she looks to you. Ask her your questions and spend some time with her.

When it is time for you to leave look into the palm of your hand and see the gift you will give her.

Your guide swims back with you to the surface and you say your goodbyes. You wade back out of the water and come back to your seated position on the beach. Spend as much time here as you need before slowly opening your eyes and bringing yourself back to this time and place.

Once you have completed this exercise, write down your experience in your journal.

Emotional Experience

When we have an emotional experience our body releases water either in the form of tears, sweat, urine or sexual secretions. Our body's response to our emotional experience is a watery one and for this reason the element of water is strongly linked to our emotions. As Sea Priestess we need to feel at one with our emotions and allow ourselves adequate and free expression. If we are to open our hearts to others then we need to understand and nurture our own emotional needs. Being emotional is often regarded as a sign of weakness but by attuning ourselves with our emotional bodies, allowing for our emotions but not becoming ruled by them we are living in a healthy way. Emotions can be the fuel for manifestation so we need to ensure that what we are feeling is honest and that we allow our emotions to flow, taking note of when we believe we are blocked or not living our lives in an emotionally honest way.

To live in an emotionally honest way we need to ensure that the lifestyle we have is in congruence. It's important that the work we do and the relationships we have support this. To look at our life with emotional honesty requires great courage because it can mean letting go of situations and people that aren't in harmony with us. When we react in an emotional way to situations it is often because another individual is reflecting back to us a lesson that we need to learn, or aspects of our behaviour, which require modification. It can be a useful exercise to do an emotional audit of your life to identify triggers and areas which are not in synch with our emotional needs. This can be done very easily by reviewing your personal journal and understanding where there are repeat patterns. For example if there are areas of your work or home life where issues happen repeatedly then this can indicate an area where there is a lack of emotional honesty. This is a difficult exercise but one that should be done on a regular basis.

The Selkie

Selkies are seal women or men found in stories from the Scottish Isles to Iceland. Their stories are associated with their sealskins which, when hidden from them or buried by them, allow them to take on human form. Their story is one of romantic tragedy, for often it tells of love lost and of the selkie disappearing from the life of a human or forced to remain when their skin is not returned to them. Their stories teach of love and of not owning the love of another. Often the selkie wife will bear children for the human but her longing for the sea is so great that it overwhelms her and when she finds her skin, she makes a break for freedom leaving behind her husband and her children. She reminds us that even in the deepest of unions, a woman needs her own space. She is the representation of freedom in love and of the feminine desire to be wild and uncontrolled. For the feminine is that which is uncontainable, like water: mutable, ebbing and flowing with the tide.

The Selkies' Story

Far far away and a long time ago in the northern lands where the sun leaves the sky for many months and the moon rules the land, there lived a man. He made his living from taking fish from the sea and selling them to his neighbours and the other townsfolk. He had been married but his wife had become sick on the birth of their child and she died, leaving him with a small scrap of a daughter who he'd fostered out to a farmer's wife who'd lost her child at the same time. He was a bitter man who lost him self at the bottom of a bottle and each time he set out for the ocean he prayed that the trip would be his last and he would be lost at sea. One summer morning when the sun ruled the land he set out in his boat, for the mackerel were schooling and there was a penny or two to be made. Alone in his boat, he laid his trace line and soon enough he was hauling them on board twenty at a time. When the buckets were full he set back inland. As he made his way back to the shore he noticed something glinting and glistening on the rocks. He couldn't take the boat too near for risk of being wrecked but his curiosity was getting the better of him, after all it could be something of value. As he strained his eyes to see it became obvious that it was just seals basking on the rocks, however he still steered the boat as near as he was able. It was then that he noticed her, as naked as a baby, waving her arms frantically from the rocks, the glinting he had seen was the light on her hair.

He shouted out to her, to wait and that he would get the boat as close as he dared before sending her a rope to haul her on board. She didn't wait for the rope but instead she jumped from the rock and the next thing he knew she was swimming alongside him and he hauled her on board. Looking down into the water he saw a flash of light and realised it was a seal's skin floating alongside her and so he pulled this out as well. Full of questions he draped her in an old jacket and asked her whatever she was doing. She didn't speak a word and he guessed she must be a foreigner thrown from a ship. She grabbed at the skin though and he took it from her locking it in the hold, it could be worth something and she owed him right enough for saving her life, not the other way around. Once at the dock he went to offload the fish and caught her with a raw one already half eaten. The poor girl must be starved. He gave her some of the bread and cheese he'd left from his breakfast. He tried to lead her off the boat but she started a racket like you'd never heard and he thought it best to leave her there in the cabin whilst he sold his catch. When he returned, he expected her to be gone but there she was, just as he'd left her and she smiled at him and again he asked her who was she. After much persistence she managed a name 'Elene'. She sure enough was a foreigner and he had no mind to be answering the questions about how he came about her, so when the sun set he walked her down to his croft. He opened the cupboard that contained his dead wife's clothes and heated a kettle for some water. "You clean yourself up" he said to her "and put on some clothes and I'll cook us some food."

And so it was she stayed with him and cooked and cleaned his home. Her language was limited but a man didn't need talking too and she supplied the comforts of the night. He got use to her manner and her being there. She had the most beautiful voice and at night he would catch her looking out to the ocean singing to it, he thought she must be homesick. Yet she never took or asked to leave. He fed her and clothed her and in return she looked after his needs and kept his home as neat as you ever saw. He noticed that her belly began to swell and soon enough she gave birth to a beautiful baby boy and they named him Cavan, for he was so bonny. Two more followed, a girl and another boy; she seemed to give birth easily and there was never a need for a midwife. When the women of the village spoke to her she was quiet and would nod and acknowledge them but she didn't mix and he liked it that way, for his business was his own. Yet as time went by she spent every night standing on the shoreline crying out to the sea and singing to the seals that basked themselves on the rocks. He couldn't make out the words but there was a lilting sadness that cried out for home and loves lost. She would take off her clothes and swim in all weathers, sometimes to the detriment of her health.

One day, Cavan was old enough to go out to the boat with him and she came down to the docks with them both, her other children attached to her skirts. He felt proud of his small family and as the neighbours waved to them he felt like he fitted in for once and realised that he didn't need the bottle like he once did and now he wanted to sail home at night and not sink to the bottom of the sea anymore. His pride in his boat and his family swelled his heart and he showed the boy all the parts of the boat, unlocking the hold to show him the treasures he kept there. As he went to tend to something leaving the boy there, Cavan picked up the sealskin and held it aloft. "Mama" he said "look at this!" Elene snatched the skin from the boy and stuffed it in her skirts, telling him to say nothing. That night when they returned to the croft, she looked down at her sleeping children and then, laying her clothes to one side, she took the sealskin and walked out down to the sea. Lifting her head she sang to the ocean of freedom and of the pain of losing her children then placing her sealskin on her body she dove into the sea and swam away. When he awoke the next day he found her gone, they searched and searched but she was never found. The children grew without a mama, the croft was un-kept and he renewed his relationship with the bottle. And the Selkie returned to the sea and mourned the children she left behind.

Notes

Notes

The Alchemy of the Sea Priestess

10

Lammas and Autumn Equinox

Lammas and the golden days of summer arrive and we move into a time of gratitude for all that we have and all that we are. In order to welcome abundance into our lives we need to let go and sacrifice those things that no longer serve our highest good. At this point in the wheel of the year we find the life-giving mother. She demonstrates a balance point of life at the time of birth, where the yonic gateway is opened as we birth the new. This is the time when we can harvest all that we have dreamt. We can manifest our lives into creation. We will give thanks and work with the bounty of water to create and manifest our live. We will work with the Goddess as Boann at Lammas and then as Yemanya at Autumn Equinox. We are working with the energies of abundance and welcoming them into our lives through the practice of gratitude.

At Lammas we will celebrate Boann, the Irish Goddess of the River Boyne. She is one of the Tuatha de Danann and her story like many of Britannia's Goddesses comes down to us through Celtic mythology. Here we find remnants of a story from the deep past, for Boann goes to the well of Seyais, which is known as the 'well of wisdom' and wishing to take that wisdom for herself she walks anti-clockwise around the well causing the waters to surge violently and rush to the sea, creating the river but drowning Boann in the process. This is the myth of the Goddess as keeper of wisdom and knowledge and she holds the land and the waters in balance. She is the creative force of new life that at times can be violent and unexpected. The peoples of the past new that the birthing of new life could be a dangerous moment for both mother and child and a balancing act between life and death.

Boann is the Goddess that we work with at this time of the year; she brings forth the life giving waters of the Boyne and yet at the same time loses her own life. Here we see the ultimate sacrifice of the life giving mother.

'A horrible pang of fear shot through me lest once again I should be called upon to sacrifice to the sea something that was becoming very dear to me. And I told the sea flat out that if it took Molly I should come after her. And it seemed to me that somewhere among the stars I heard faint laughter, silver laughter and I knew that the Goddess was glad and this was the sound of Her joy, for I had offered the acceptable sacrifice without which no mating can be consecrated to the Great Goddess. For in every union the woman makes this offer, for she goes down to the gates of death to open them to the incoming life, and shall not the man, in common justice match her giving? For without the shedding of blood there is no redemption whether in childbed or upon the field of battle, both crucifixions after their kind, and both of redeeming power when made sacramental by an ideal.' (*The Sea Priestess,* Dion Fortune pg 227).

The act of childbirth is full of danger for both mother and child and life is held in balance at this point. One of the most disturbing concepts to come to grips with within Fortune's *The Sea Priestess* is the concept of sacrifice. There are many references to this within the book and it is one of the deeper esoteric lessons that she is trying to impart. As they explore the past with the Priest of the Moon, they learn that the Atlantean Sea Priestess is called to Britannia to sacrifice men to the sea for it is threatening to overwhelm the land. Wilfred dreams of when, in a past life, chosen as the sacrifice to the sea, for his last wish he had asked for the Sea Priestess. After much debate the wish is given but torture is given as a punishment. The Wilfred of the past must drown without being given the drugged wine, yet in return he has the Sea Priestess and in this bliss he finds that she is all women and he is all men. Later in the book as they restore the temple for Morgan the builders disabled son 'the Mooncalf' is taken as a sacrifice by the sea when, he falls into a culvert and is lost. The current day Wilfred also worries that the sea will take him in an act of ultimate sacrifice for his work with Morgan.

The definition of sacrifice is 'a surrender of something of value in order to gain something more desirable'. *(Collins English Dictionary)* The concept of sacrifice is often muddied through past historical acts whereby it is associated with the ritual killing of an animal or even a human in order to appease a God/Goddess. The hanged man tarot card is a good starting point for understanding the concept of sacrifice and how it can be interpreted in relation to gaining deeper understanding of our-self and our spiritual development. In the tarot card the man is hanging upside down, blinded in one eye *(Ryder Waite tarot deck)*. The sacrifice he is making though, is a willing one as he has realised that he is close to gaining a greater consciousness that cannot be gained by physical or intellectual effort. It involves sacrificing his existing beliefs and habits, to allow for new ones to rise to the surface. It is a complete surrender of his defences and all of the things that he believes have given him control within his life. This is the blind leap in the dark. Here he can act on faith alone and he is suspended between one form of life and another. He is at his most vulnerable.

In Fortune's book, the past life Wilfred trades an easy death for the knowing of the Sea Priestess. Sacrifice therefore requires us to enter the deepest state of surrender, where we are unsure as to what may happen but where we know in our hearts that in sacrificing our beliefs and ideals we can attain something much greater and of deeper value.

Sacrifice teaches us about the inherent laws of nature, in that one thing must die for another to live, to eat we must take the life of another whether that is an animal or a plant. This is true for all that exists within the natural world and here it is our deepest held beliefs about our self and our place in the world that we are relinquishing in order to find the divine within. This is a sacrifice that requires no blood or loss of life but instead a loss of the artificial self, the ego, so that we can see more clearly.

At Lammas we need to surrender those things, which no longer serve our highest ideals. We need to decide where we need to let go of our beliefs in order for new ones to take their place. This is the traditional teaching where we learn the lesson of the grain, that it must be cut in order for us to survive.

A new life beckons and it is now that we must sacrifice those things we hold dear but which are taking up space in our heads and our hearts and not allowing the new to enter. Our attachment to things that no longer serve, such as our aches and pains, our weight issues or our bad relationships, can be very strong and we may need assistance through healing sessions or counseling to remove our attachments. We must learn to recognise those things in order that we can work to release them. We can do this through counselling or talking therapy, however we can also do this through movement in the body and the breath. By working with our breath we can release deep-seated attitudes. In the simple act of changing the way we breathe we can teach our body and in turn our minds to accept new ways of being.

Exercise of Surrender

In this exercise you are going to surrender your old ways of thinking, those bad habits that you have incorporated into your life that no longer serve you. This could be that self-criticizing voice or any form of toxic thought that holds you back and stops you from fulfilling your true potential. To do this you will work with the breath, cleansing your mind and allowing your true potential. It is your reactive mind that produces negative thoughts. When you are confronted with ideas or beliefs that make you feel uncomfortable, you can react with anger, frustration, guilt or aggression. You need to allow for this reaction but not to incorporate it. You shouldn't allow it to become part of your story. Allow the thought but do not take heed of it. You can tell when you become anxious or frustrated because it is your breath that changes. It acts as a signal to tell you that something is wrong. When you are aware of your breath you are given an early warning system that tells you to heed your mind and your body. It tells you that something is wrong. You can vary your breathing and your body will react accordingly. So if your breath is a cleansing and detoxifying breath, your mind and your body react to cleanse and detoxify your system. The breath is a great non-verbal communicator and your body's way of knowing where it is.

To practice surrender you are going to use a cleansing fire breath, which will awaken the Kundalini energy within your base chakra, allowing it to rise through your chakras releasing the energy through your crown. This is a very cleansing and detoxifying breath. Kundalini energy is the snake or fire energy that lives within the fourthth vertebrae of the spine.

In most people it remains inactive but in awakening the Kundalini energy you can enter a state of bliss and can experience an awakening of inner knowledge, thus allowing you to recognize and work with the attachments you have in your life. It is the base energy and the very essence of all life. It is the Snake Goddess energy, sometimes known as Kundalini Shakti. It ascends through the spinal column, upwards through the spinal nerve endings, rising and clearing blockages and the subtle body as it moves towards the crown chakra. It is the cosmic source energy and in awakening it you can feel in touch with the Goddess within and without and like Wilfred you can experience the bliss of being all that is.

Physical symptoms can occur on awakening the Kundalini energy. (*Kundalini and the Chakras evolution in this lifetime a practical guide,* Genevieve Lewis Paulson). If you live in a heart centered way and perform the grounding exercises afterwards to disperse the energy, then any physical symptoms should be minor. If Kundalini spontaneously arises during any exercise you are performing then the grounding exercises in Chapter two will help enormously.

To begin with, arrange your central altar for where you will perform the exercise, putting a candle and something to light it with in front of where you will be sitting. Ground and centre and then, as in previous exercises call the Goddess of the wheel into the space where you are seated. Sit cross legged on the floor, or seated on a chair if this is not possible, and then slowly swinging your arms from side to side twist at the waist, do this for about two minutes. If you feel any sharp pain in the spine then stop and just do the breathing exercise. Now stop twisting and, concentrating on the third eye (the point between the eyebrows), start to breathe through your nose in short sharp breaths, like sniffing, for about one minute. Repeat the twisting and the sniffing three times. Then lighting the candle sit for a moment looking at the flame and imagine a fiery image at the base of your spine. Move this fire energy you have awakened up your spine imagining it rising up through each of your chakras until it is released through the crown. Feel yourself bathed in this wonderful fiery energy, which moves down showering your body from your crown chakra with beautiful, healing, golden light. Finally when you are ready feel the energy dissipating and moving back down through the spine until eventually it returns back to the base. Then lie on the floor in a relaxation pose and imagine any excess energy returning to the Earth. Feel yourself attached once again to Mother Earth fully grounded and in total surrender.

This is a very powerful exercise which can be performed on its own, however to raise the Kundalini energy within the body then it is also recommended that you practice

Kundalini yoga. Yogi Bhajan taught this form of yoga for the first time in the West during the 1960's and it can be life changing. There are many classes and media available to assist you in understanding these wonderful techniques.

Autumn Equinox

Yemanya is a Brazilian/African Goddess, she is an Orisha and a Goddess of abundance and manifestation. She is often depicted as a mermaid and is associated with the wide expansiveness of the oceans. She is an all-giving mother Goddess who protects children and mothers. In Brazilian culture her festivals are at Imbolc and at Summer Solstice. Here we celebrate her in the autumn for she is 'in my vision' a Goddess of ripeness and the abundance that is within our oceans. Her name is Yey Omo Eja, which means 'mother whose children are the fish'. She gives birth to and manifests our desires as she gives birth to the abundance of the ocean.

Often in life we can experience many desires but the act of bringing these into form eludes us. We are unable to manifest them into our daily lives. We can believe that luck, fate or destiny are such that these things are not for us. Yet in knowing what it is we truly desire and being honest with ourselves about what these things are, in working with our true natures we can bring into form all that we desire. We live in an abundant universe that does not limit or ration our desires. What we require though is clarity of thought about those things that we do desire. Often the 'things' we believe we need are masking the deeper requirements we have. So a desire for money can mask the real desire for security and safety within our world, or the need to make choices that better reflect our inner emotional state. We can encourage abundance into our lives through the practice of gratitude.

The act of expressing gratitude in our lives means that we approach life not from a place of entitlement but from a place of humility and of knowing that we are working in harmony with our divine spirit selves. We are telling the universe that we appreciate the things we have in our lives and that we would like to encourage more of those things. When we give thanks for our bodies, our families and our lives we immediately recognise those things that are important to us. Gratitude assists us in identifying those things that truly matter and our desires are then matched with those things that make us grateful and ultimately that make us fulfilled and happy.

In expressing gratitude we should try and do so on a regular basis. This will help us to keep in touch with what is working in our lives and making us happy. On waking in the morning it is good to express gratitude as part of an affirmation. This can be done while looking in the mirror. Something as simple as:

'I am so grateful for my beautiful smile and the wonderful nights sleep I had.'

If you smile at yourself in the mirror it will automatically make you feel better, and even if you did not get a great nights sleep you are telling the universe that this is what makes you happy. I also find it's useful to keep a gratitude page in my diary where I write down the things I feel happy about. Gratitude should be a spontaneous reaction to all of the things you have in your life. Even when your life is not going so well, all of us can still find things to be grateful for.

As well as practicing gratitude on a daily basis, we can also more formally express those things in our lives for which we are grateful by performing a gratitude ceremony. As part of this ceremony we are going to take a Shamanic journey to meet with Yemanya and thank her for her abundant nature, whilst at the same time receive her individual message to us. This is an important journey that can focus our attention on to what is important in our lives and allow us the time to listen to our inner voice and recognize what makes us content.

Gratitude Journey

In order to do this ceremony you will need to gather together the following items for the shamanic journey you will make. You will need to have a recording of either a slow drumbeat or the sound of the sea and tide. You are using this sound to change your sense of consciousness, allowing you to make this journey. You will also need the following:

- Items for your altar that represent things you are grateful for; these could be pictures of family, friends or representations of the same
- Something to represent the elements
- Your chalice and drinking water
- Music of the sounds of the sea or a slow drum beat
- Paper and pen

As in all the previous ceremonies, ground and centre and call the energies of the Goddess into the space. Then begin to set up your altar by first putting the elements in the directions. As you do so, take each element and thank the Goddess for this element. So, for example, as you place your symbol of air, thank the Goddess for your life breath, for clean air, for the birds of the air, for wisdom and knowledge. Thank the Goddess for your mind and your thoughts. Then as you move to fire do the same, thank the Goddess for the warmth of your home, for the fuel you use to cook your food, thank her for your creativity and your optimism. Then placing the water on the altar, thank the Goddess for the clean water you drink, for the beautiful places of water such as the oceans and the rivers. Thank her for your emotional life and for the beauty and compassion there is in your life. Finally place your earth symbol and thank the Goddess for the food you eat, for this beautiful planet, thank her for all of the wonderful things that manifest in your life.

Once you have placed all your elements on the altar, say thank you for all of the elements that make up all of the form on this planet. Then, taking your items, place them one by one on the altar taking time to express your gratitude for each one.

Start the music and lie on the floor, closing your eyes and putting yourself into a relaxed state. Imagine yourself walking towards a door, you are entering the non-ordinary world; behind this door lies a beautiful beach and the ocean. Look around the beach taking time to familiarize yourself with your surroundings. You will need to meet with your guide. Notice if there are any animals, people or elementals on the beach, recognise your guide who is waiting for you. Talk with them for a while and get to know them, listen to any messages they may have for you and tell them you wish to meet with Yemanya to thank her for the things you have in your life. Then when you are ready go with them to meet her. Imagine how she looks to you and where you go to meet her. Does she come to the beach? Or do you enter the water? How do you feel meeting this amazing mother Goddess? Tell her about all of the things in your life for which you are grateful. Listen to what she has to say to you and how you feel. When you are ready to leave, thank her for her wisdom and finding a gift in your pocket give it to her. Allow yourself to return to the beach and your guide and thank them for their assistance. Then, leaving the beach, return back through the door and slowly bring yourself back into the room. Turning off the music take the paper and pen and write down your journey. Rather like the dream state it is a good idea to do this immediately as you will find the memory of the journey will fade.

Remember on each day during this period to say thank you for all that you have in your life.

Magical Creatures of the Seas

There is much mythology surrounding the seas, lakes and oceans of this world. Mermaids, selkies, water nymphs, undines, giant octopus, the Loch Ness monster, sea dragons and kelpies; all of these creatures live in a mythological underworld told of in children's tales and glimpsed through the veil by sailors and fishermen. Their stories reveal much about our wonder of the deep, for even though we have visited the moon we have never been to the deepest part of the ocean and it may well contain secrets that are still to be uncovered. The creatures of the very deepest seas are alien beyond imagination because of the pressure exerted at that depth and because the sunlight on which we all thrive cannot reach down that far.

In this chapter we will explore some of the ancient tales of the deep and discover the healing power of the dolphins and whales that swim in the seas: Yemanya's creatures. Through these magical animals we can find parts of our selves that have been lost and we can utilise their stories in meditation and self-healing.

Mythological Sea Creatures

Mermaids

Half fish, half woman; the mermaid is the feminine symbol of mystery and freedom. She is an enchantress luring men to their deaths in the deep ocean through the power of her voice. She crosses cultural barriers and there are tales of mermaids the world over. She is aligned with the magical nature of women and their deep intuitive nature. Her top half represents mother love, bare breasted and giving, and her bottom half the primal part of our nature, ancient and prehistoric. In stories she is often portrayed as dangerous and 'like the Selkie' her tale is often one of romantic tragedy. She grants the wishes of men and in doing so often sacrifices that which is dear to her. Her tale is one of love and in most versions she falls in love with a human man, and either he or she must sacrifice all that they hold dear (the land or the sea) for their love to continue. Her story is one of living in two worlds and how these cannot be reconciled with one another to true satisfaction.

From the tales of the mermaid we can learn of desire, freedom and the reconciliation of opposing natures. She teaches us to live with freedom and to push aside those barriers that stop us from being all that we can be. She is willing to sacrifice all that she has in order to find love and herself. Her's is a tale of the magic of transforming the self.

The mermaid has the power to divine the future and her name derives from 'mere' which means lake. The mermaid is a Lady of the Lake or a Lady of the Water. She is the subconscious impulse that lies within us all, that lives with the mother Goddess. We return to her at the time of death and she rules all that is eternal and everlasting. In mermaid tales she is often immortal and drinks ambrosia, the nectar of the Gods that bestows everlasting life. The mermaid is beautiful but treacherous 'as is the sea' and she teaches us that in beauty we can find deceit.

The earliest known story of a mermaid is that of the Syrian Goddess Atargatis who was in love with a shepherd and accidentally killed him. Feeling remorseful she jumped into a lake to take the form of a fish but the lake would not conceal her beauty and so she became half fish, half woman. This was very similar to the Babylonian Goddess Ea who the Sea Priestess sings of. The Goddess as mermaid is the primordial Goddess of the ancients, represented by the fish Goddess. We are connected to the waters of this earth and the mermaid is a representation of this connection. Mermaids capture our imagination and there are also many modern representations of them in art and film. This enduring fascination reveals a deep routed need in our psyches to explore all that they have to offer.

Sirens

Sirens were spirits of the sea who had the heads of beautiful women but the bodies of birds. Again they are ancient depictions of the Neolithic Goddesses, who were often depicted as fish or birds. They are associated with death and it is their voice that deceives men, leading them onto the rocks and drowning them. They are often shown with human skeletons and are associated with, Scylla and Charybdis, monsters of the deep. The expression 'out of the frying pan into the fire' is a good depiction of these monsters for Scylla is a six-headed monster with triple rows of teeth and Charybdis is a whirlpool that can sink the largest of ships. In avoiding one it may well be that you get drawn into the other. They are the representations of choice and of the change that is life, which is inevitable.

Water Nymphs/Undine

Water nymphs are traditionally associated with rivers, springs and lakes. They are generally benevolent elementals but they also warn of tricksters and of deception. The word 'nymph' means 'young girl' and it is nymphs who are the guardians of the springs and wells and who can grant our wishes. Even today we throw coins in fountains for good luck. In Greek mythology there were three types of water nymph: Oceanids who were the sea nymphs, Naiad who were the fountain and spring nymphs and Nerieds who were associated with the warm waters of the Mediterranean.

Water nymphs represent the ancient Goddess of the springs and wells. These were the openings of the Earth, the Goddesses' vulva, and were places of special significance and sacred to her people not least for the fresh water they often supplied. In some respect nymphs are similar to fairies in that they live in nature and represent our natural instinctive natures. They can teach us to follow our true nature and to live in tune with the beauty of the Earth and its waters. They ask us to look at the parts of ourselves that need healing through spending time in nature.

An undine is a water nymph of Teutonic heritage and she is known for her ability to curse. She does this when wronged in love. In her tale she loses her looks after giving birth to her children and her man falls into the arms of another. This is a story of a mythological creature who experiences loss and takes her revenge through her curse, which causes the man to never be able to sleep without losing consciousness and dying. Yet in this curse she loses what she holds dear, for to live without sleep is impossible. The myth also says that to gain a soul the undine must marry a human man and bear his child. The undine teaches that in revenge we can hurt ourselves as much as another and in doing so lose ourselves.

Kelpie

The kelpie is a water horse whose skin is black and its mane constantly dripping wet. Its skin is like that of a seal but cold as death to the touch. It is known for enticing young children into water by offering rides on its back, only to drag them down into the water and drown them. It has Celtic and Nordic derivations and is also known as a sea glass pony due to its beauty distracting the onlooker. They are wraiths of the deep, stealing lives away. The kelpie has been associated with other lake monsters such as the Loch Ness monster. It has webbed feet and a tail like a fish. There are many tales of sea serpents, dragons and horses in myth and legend and it is likely they have similar ancestry. It may be that there is some historic truth to these legends and the creatures described are prehistoric animals that survived long after their relatives, the dinosaurs. Kelpies teach us about self-awareness and to not be distracted by what seems beautiful on the surface but which may be deadly underneath. They teach us about substance over form.

Healing Power of Whales and Dolphins

Dolphins, whales and porpoises are all sea mammals that give birth to live young and need to breathe oxygen in order to survive. They live in the ocean but are warm blooded. They are found all over the world and evolved around ten million years ago. They are known for their playfulness, intelligence and their song. There are many resources available to study and understand these beautiful mammals. However one of their unique qualities is their ability to heal, through touch and through their song. Dolphins in particular have become associated with their healing abilities. Part of the reason for this is their *joie de vivre* and their innate playful natures. They are also highly intelligent evolved mammals with social interaction and hierarchies within their 'pods'. The dolphin is a great teacher of living life in the present moment and shows us how to live in a holistic and an environmentally sustainable way. Their social natures are complex and they are able to communicate with each other and us in an almost telepathic way.

Dolphin energy is heart opening and allows for the flow and joy of movement within the body and in our preconception of the self. Their healing powers can be physical, mental or spiritual and they are the all round mind, body and soul healers. Their energetic frequency is at a much higher level than most people and as such when we come into contact with them they can make us feel uplifted and spiritually more in-tune both with nature and ourselves. When people swim or are near dolphins their spirits are raised in both the literal and the metaphoric sense.

As we study dolphins more we are realising how intelligent they are and also how their intelligence is displayed through creative right brain thinking, rather than the logical left brain approach we often take as humans. In developing our creative and intuitive selves we are able to access the healing and the emotional intelligence displayed by dolphins.

Dolphins also use sonar to enable their healing abilities, their song triggers the production of T-cells and endorphins, which bring about harmony between the left and right sides of the brain. The energy from the sonar also resonates in the bones causing a phenomenon called cavitations inside the soft body tissue. These low frequency sound waves cause changes at the molecular level within the body, healing tissue and dissolving cancerous lumps and tumors. The Sea Priestesses of old used these same techniques for healing in Atlantis, and dolphins still have these techniques today. In modern science we are only just learning of the beneficial effects of sound healing.

Whale song can also be used to harness these sound healing techniques and the song of whales is often played to aid sleep and meditation. Our bodies are made up of energy, and sound waves can permeate our cells cleansing and healing them and allowing cell repair. We can use instruments to create these sounds, however the sounds in nature such as the whale song can be used to equal or greater benefit. As well as benefiting the body, sound can also change our mood and perception of what is around us. If we live in a built up area with a lot of traffic noise then whale song can be played to bring us back into nature and still our minds. It is also believed that whale song can bring deep healing to the planet as well as to humans. Their song is the song of the Goddess Gaia and the planetary vibration would not be the same without the songs of the whales travelling around her, soothing and healing her earthly body.

The meditation below is a meditation to allow you to find your own Sea Priestess song. You will meet with the dolphins and receive their blessing and your song. It is recommended that you tape the meditation or get someone else to read it for you so that you can become fully immersed.

Finding Your Song

Make yourself comfortable either sitting or lying. Keep warm by placing a shawl or wrap over your body. You want to feel comfortable enough for sleep and to get into that state of mind that we achieve just prior to falling asleep. If you do go to sleep during this meditation don't worry, as this is most likely what your body needs at this time and you will find that your song comes to you over the next few days as it has been embedded in your subconscious.

Close your eyes and start to relax by taking some deep breaths, move your mind through your body noticing where there may be any aches or tension. Breathe into these parts and release what is there. Feel yourself sinking into your chair or the floor. Allow any thoughts but let them pass. Concentrate on listening to your breath.

Imagine that you are on a boat, not too far out to sea as you can still see the coast. It is a beautiful calm and sunny day and you feel completely relaxed and safe on the boat. Hear the water as it splashes up against the sides, and the movement as it rocks back and forth in the water. You are curious to look into the water and you move towards the boats railings and look over the side. As you do so a grey nose juts up above the water line and a bottle nosed dolphin looks up at you. Then one more, then another until there are nine dolphins all swimming next to the boat and watching you as you watch them. They then begin a water display for you, diving in and out of the water, splashing you as they come near to the boat. Telepathically one of them asks you to join them and without fear you jump off of the boat into the water. You realise that you can swim as easily as they can and you leap out of the water in your excitement, diving back under you can see the sea bed and all of the fish beneath you.

Three of the dolphins swim next to you and, pushing you along, you all swim in formation together diving in and out of the water and gliding beneath its surface. Play with the dolphins and feel their healing energy surge through you as you abandon yourself to play and enjoy. If there are parts of you that need specific healing or you have any aches and pains, which you wish to release allow the dolphins to work with you to heal them.

One of the dolphins then swims next you and he places his nose against your third eye. You hear your song reverberate through your body, through your skeletal structure, your muscle fibre and tissue. This is your song, your wisdom returned to you from the water and from ancient memory. It has been held in safekeeping by the dolphins for millennia.

Thank the dolphin for returning your song to you, stay with them and play in the water for as long as you wish.

When you are ready to depart say goodbye to the dolphins and find yourself back on board the boat. Next to you are buckets of fish so throw them into the water for the dolphins as a thank you. Slowly come back into your body feeling your feet and your hands and when you are ready, open your eyes. Remember to drink lots of water over the next few days and you will find that your song will come to you as words and music. Write this down as you receive it and begin to sing it often, especially when next to the water. If any parts of your song are unclear you can return to this mediation until you fully understand your song.

Finding your song goes much deeper though than the meditation. It is the essential soul path of the Sea Priestess. It is her magic and her enchantment. She sings of her desires, her loves, her wisdom and inner knowing. She sings to the land and to the sea and the land and the sea sings back to her in return. When she sings her song is woven into the fabric of all the songs that have preceded it and it is held in the collective memory.

When in nature, it requires that you listen to the world around you. To the man made sounds and the sounds of nature. So often in our lives we are so busy talking amongst ourselves, or our mind chatter is so loud that we don't truly listen to the natural world. If you choose to listen then all of nature's secrets are revealed. By listening and allowing your throat chakra to fully open you can allow the sounds of nature to flow through you and be revealed in your own song.

Finding your song in nature

It is necessary to be outdoors to do this exercise and if you can to be by the sea or a body of water, (or anywhere in nature if this is not possible). Ground and centre yourself and call in the Goddesses of the season or the centre. Allow your awareness to expand around you. Listen to all of the sounds that you can hear. Listen and feel the air as it touches your skin. Notice the sensation of the elements, earth, air, fire (sun) and water. Allow your awareness to expand as far out as possible to encompass as much of the natural environment as you can. Feel your feet connected and rooted to the Earth from your heart, and your heart and crown connected to the sky above. Radiate your heart energy out into the environment and feel it connect with the natural world. Make a soul connection with the land, with the sea, with the air. Listen deeply and further than you would normally. Then sound out vocally the sounds of which you are aware. You may find that the sounds are disconnected or you may find that words of a song come to you, it doesn't matter just go with what comes.

Progressively as you develop this exercise you will experience your own song and the song of nature becoming entwined and complimenting one another. You may feel a little awkward at first but you will be surprised at the depth of connection that can be made doing this exercise.

Natural magic

When experiencing the natural realm you are also working with the magical realms and with the elementals and spirit. You are working with the invisible, the place of dreams and of the imagination.

You become able to visualise and develop something that does not yet exist in the material world.

Magic is the realm of the idea and the inspiration. There is paradox; you are acting in the present yet visualising and holding in your mind a projection of your future self, your ideas and creations. In the chaotic world even small changes can cause complexity to the system. This holds true for our lives as well, where small changes to the way in which we act can have complex outcomes. Within this chaotic system though are patterns and harmonies that play out, and the Sea Priestess acknowledges these truths and strives to understand her own circumstances and patterns. She knows that control is an illusion and instead rides the wave of change knowing that she will reach her destination regardless of the outer chaos she may experience.

In experiencing your creativity and your imagination within the moment you can breathe life into the projects and artistic goals you have. You are limitless in what you can achieve. All of us have a huge capacity towards greatness but rather than striving for this through the accumulation of things, or acting out the goals of others, we can harness this ability by letting go and living in the moment. You can breath life into your dreams and experience the fullness of who you can become. You are utilising natural magic as well as the magic of intention.

In this chapter there is an invitation to do an exercise to increase your ability to concentrate and focus on an image and hold that image in your minds eye.

To find your future self and your Sea Priestess song you need to have a clear image of what that looks like. You need to be able to see it, smell it and taste it. It has to be as real in your imagination as if it already existed. To do this you need to use your imagination.

As children we all have an inbuilt imagination. We can imagine worlds from simple objects. A cardboard box can be a pirate ship, a castle or a spaceship. We can visualise ourselves as a champion, princess or an astronaut. Lots of children create whole imaginary worlds peopled with characters from their own and others imaginations. As we move into adulthood the practical world of form takes over and we dismiss imagination as the realm of children. Or else we turn our imagination into unreal expectations of a future we are unprepared to work on as 'real' life takes all our time and energy.

So it's important to rediscover that imaginative place within your self. You need to ignite that creative part of your mind that can imagine the spectacular. To do this you should start a creative or artistic pursuit. You may not be an artist but you can be creative. Surround yourself with artistic images, the wilder the better. Listen to music you wouldn't normally listen to. Get in touch with your dream world. You should have already done this if you have worked through the exercises, in previous chapters. Be exposed to as many creative images as possible to ignite that part of your brain.

You can then use this information to start to visualise your dreams, goals and creative projects. Once you are clear on this you can then start on building the ability to hold the image in your mind.

Candle exercise

This is a master exercise in concentration because it is very simple but very powerful. This exercise should be done in a dark room as the candle will then be the only illumination in the space. (Take care around lighted candles and place the candle in a safe place away from fabrics or combustible materials). Sitting comfortably either upright in a chair or cross-legged on the floor, light a candle in front of you, a long taper candle works well for this, and then begin to gaze at the candle. Watch as the flame changes shape. Allow your vision to blur continuously looking at the candle. See the shapes the candle flame makes and when you are ready close your eyes, still visualising the candle in your minds eye.

Looking all the time through your sixth chakra (third eye). If you cannot see the candle open your eyes and continue to look until you can hold the image of the candle in your mind. When you are comfortable with this, start to move the flame, making it grow and then become smaller again. When you are ready open your eyes and do the same with the candle in front of you. With practice you will be able to move the flame in your mind and in front of you.

This exercise is a key to concentrating the mind. When you are able to move the candle in this way, start to visualise other objects. You are working towards visualising and imagining your dreams as if they have already happened.

Concentration is an essential skill to practice and you should do so regularly. If you have problems concentrating and closing down the mind chatter use your breath and relaxation exercises before starting.

It is also important that that the energy you experience is grounded out into the world. In honouring and respecting nature, it is necessary that we act this way in our daily lives, as well as in our spiritual practices. For the Sea Priestess this means respecting and working with the natural environment and supporting others to do so.

There are many organisations that have been set up to protect the environment and the oceans, and by supporting them either through financial sponsorship, voluntary work, or by assisting in campaigns you can make a real difference, and your song travels out in a very practical way.

Notes

Notes

11

Immersion as a Sea Priestess

'If you make yourself a Priestess...meditate upon the moon. She will awaken your womanhood and lend you power. May the great Goddess bless you and help you.' (*The Sea Priestess,* Dion Fortune Pg 205)

As you have journeyed these past months you have meditated on the moon in all her different aspects, from new through to dark. You have seen how the phases of the moon have impacted your body and the ebb and flow of your emotional and creative state. You have lived close to nature and found your own cycle mirrored and reflected back to you. You have made home altars and decorated them with the items that reflect the seasons and your dreams, connecting deeply with the watery Goddesses of your land. You have received your Sea Priestess song. Within this journey you have been able to create your life and you have seen how this allows you to surrender to what will be and live within the present moment.

The journey is a reflection and a mirror into which you can look and find your true self. You started your journey with all that you needed, because all of the qualities required are found internally. All of the sacred objects that you have collected, the altars you have built, are merely reflections of your inner self that you have brought out into the world so that you can see them, touch them and know them for yourself.

The way of the Sea Priestess is a path that constantly changes, growing and maturing over time, spiralling into the future. Sometimes it is possible to feel that you are very close to her and your calling and at others far removed and distant, yet this is all part of the same path. The path of the Sea Priestess is like a labyrinth twisting and turning yet always taking you further into yourself. It is a path of dreaming your world into existence and this dream is ever changing, ebbing and flowing like the tide.

It is a path of study and of learning and this book is just a signpost to start you on your journey. How you navigate that journey and walk your path is your own; and it is the wonder and the mystery of this and the places that it can take you that are as myriad as life itself. Now is the time when the real journey begins. When you decide whether you wish to continue to learn and to dream and to follow the path of Sea Priestess, or whether your journey will take you elsewhere. This is a decision that only you can make and whatever the decision is, it will be the right one for you.

If you decide to dedicate your life to this path it is a personal prayer that is between you and Goddess. You are not dedicating yourself to another person, to a thing or to a cause. Rather you are speaking out-loud your intention for how you wish to live your life and how you will share your love of life and of her with others. Your dedication may be very simple in its expression. You may want to live your life close to nature or to help clean her oceans and seas by working with others. You may desire to express your creative nature more through art or music. You may wish to make remembering her part of your day, lighting a candle on your altar and saying a daily prayer. Your dedication is as simple or as complicated as you wish to make it. When we speak words of dedication the universe and the Goddess will challenge us with the decision we have made. We will never be challenged more than we can cope with, but your dedication will change your life. She changes everything she touches and everything she touches changes.

In making a decision to walk the path of the Sea Priestess you are connecting with ancient energies and yet at the same time you are creating the Sea Priestess of the future/your future. You need to be clear about what that means and what your goals and aspirations are for your path. Yet at the same time you are entering the un-knowing for you cannot know where your actions will lead.

However much we may believe that we are ready to dedicate our lives to a path and a way of being, we can often feel unworthy of the goals that we set ourselves, this can be particularly true of a path such as the Sea Priestess in that we are calling ourselves something and practicing a path that is little recognised or understood in the modern world. This requires courage and self-belief and it is not a choice to be made lightly. It requires surrendering to the decision and allowing it to be what it will be.

You can, if you wish, make this dedication within a specially prepared ceremony. Creating a personal dedication ceremony can mark the start of your journey as a Sea Priestess, it can be a way of acknowledging both to yourself and others that you are making changes in your life. It can be deeply personal without reference to the external world or something that you share with others.

In creating your ceremony do so in a sacred way and in a way that has meaning for you. Speak your own words that you have given time and thought to prepare. If it includes other people they should never be coerced into taking part in something or speaking words that they have not prepared themselves or do not understand. Any self-dedication ceremony is powerful and should be given reverence and respect. I have not included an example as it is a powerful lesson to create this wonderful ceremony for yourself using all you have learnt so far. As you deepen and grow in this work you can make this ceremony many times, each time bringing to it all that you have learnt and experienced.

Sacred relationships

Some readers of this book who are familiar with Dion Fortunes work may be disappointed that I have not looked at the relationship between men and woman in the exercises and that the polarity and energy exchange hinted at within the novel have been missed. I do recognise that this part of the novel is an important part of the Sea Priestess story, and believe its origins lie within the sacred practice of tantra. However I believe that it is with the transformation of the self that we embody the path of the Sea Priestess, and access these teachings.

The word 'tantra' comes from the Sanskrit 'tanoti' which means to expand and it has at its heart the two principles in creation, the primal male initiating energy which embodies consciousness and light and is the purusha,

Shivic energy and the feminine of becoming and bringing forth creation, which is prakriti or Shakti energy. Within the book I have addressed the idea of 'energy' and how the world we experience can be understood through experiencing and recognising our own energies and how we interact with the natural world. I have also covered the ideas, of concentration and conscious intent. I have concentrated on the Yin energy, the feminine and the receptive nature of this energy. What I have not covered in any detail is the polarity between male and female.

In the novel Wilfred and Morgan Le Fay work together to realise the culmination of their two energies in an act of magic that results in her disappearance. In accessing this energy I hope I have shown that it can be an inner practice as well as one that involves a partner. Everything is energy so in directing and transforming that energy you can simultaneously be both divinely feminine and masculine. Taking this outside of the self to encompass a partner it is necessary to recognise the polarity and to explore the relationship at an energetic level. This is not just about the sexual relationship, but the energetic one, and the erotic expression of the self in whatever forms that may take. Understanding polarity and the freedom to express this within a relationship is a tool for sustaining communication and for understanding the archetypes that are being expressed.

To ask another to take on board the archetype of the Sea Priestess within a relationship where they may not understand the energetic resonance can be egocentric and limiting to the relationship. Therefore in this self-transformational work we are dealing with our own embodiment of the divine and not exploring polaric relationships with others.

In transcending the personal and accessing your divine nature both the masculine and the feminine; then the worlds of spirit and matter can be combined, body and soul and there will be positive impacts on all of your relationships.

My own journey

In deepening this work I have had to move ever closer to Goddess and my relationship with her. It has been challenging and I have come up against resistances of both a practical and spiritual nature. Not least that in outwardly naming myself Priestess I have given myself a high ideal to live up to; high ideals that I do not always meet.

We all live in a time of paradox where we often have to carry two opposing thoughts in our minds, not least that in our individuality we are also part of a greater whole that knows no separation. I am like many people learning to be spiritual in a practical and material world, and to cope with the challenges this brings. Not least that we have now reached the tipping point from a global climatic perspective. The world of tomorrow will be a very different one from the one we inhabit today. We are going to have to relearn the skills of living in community and understand that our contribution is a part of the whole, and, that to be whole everyone needs to feel valued in their contribution. We will need to learn to be self-sufficient and not rely on government to satisfy our needs; and we are already having to learn that the 'material stuff' we thought made our lives whole was an illusion and that to live well is to live light. For me this is as challenging a concept as it is for the next person. How can I live the life I love which involves, travel and car ownership and a love of eating out etc with protecting a world whose resources are being used up and where climate and structural reform are desperately needed. I certainly don't feel I have the answers, however I do believe that in following the path I have set myself that the answers will come as they are relevant to me and the lives of the people I reach out and connect with.

Through all of these challenges I am constantly required to negotiate my personal relationships, my relationship with spirit and my relationship with the land. To be whole I know I need wholeness in these relationships. In deepening my connection with Goddess as Mother Earth it is showing and teaching me what needs to be done. Not just in my life but within my wider community. As we are all awakening to these truths we are inspiring each other to lead greater more 'truthful' lives that express our connection.

I truly believe that love really does conquer all, and as I set out to master what is to come, to innovate and ultimately create this new world, I hold love at my centre and radiate it out from my heart chakra knowing that it will provide me with a compass and clear direction.

In my own practice I work to regain wholeness and balance. My intention is to balance my own energy so that I can act in the world and bring forth my creativity. This means finding time for creativity, time for spiritual activity, time for work and rest and time to be joyful and playful. Understanding my heart's song and knowing my path assists in this balance because I can channel my energy into what really makes my heart sing. I can say no to projects and causes that don't inspire me. I can work with people who make me feel magnificent and vice versa. I can choose to do what I am here to do and do it with heart, soul, body and mind fully engaged.

Sometimes I am unsuccessful but I am steadily beginning to recognise those times and understanding where I need to change course. The ancient Atlantean Sea Priestesses understood how to chart their course; they were after all exceptional navigators. The teachings that they bring allow me to understand my receptivity, to find balance and to connect with the land and the ocean. They allow me to activate the memory of water and to use its healing power to heal my own life.

It seems such a simple concept to act in the present and yet most of the time we do not actively engage with it. I know myself that I set to do lists of tasks that require my attention and then tick them off as I accomplish them, adding new ones as I go. Knowing that I will feel happy and content when I have done these things. Projecting my happiness into a future that has yet to arrive.

I spent many years projecting myself into the future. Today was never quite good enough for me. There was always something that I needed to do in order that my tomorrow would be better. I never once thought that maybe tomorrow could be worse as I am by nature an optimist as our most human beings. It is part of the human nature and psyche to not want to associate our past behaviour with negative outcomes and to see our future as better, than the present moment. Which is why so many of us continue to overeat, drink too much, or smoke, and continue our destructive habits that our destroying our planet. We find it hard to associate our behaviour with the outcome, e.g. becoming overweight or suffering from conditions associated with our actions. In projecting our futures we optimistically hope that 'if I just had' or 'if I…', you can add anything here; 'I will be happy'. I am gradually discovering though that this type of thinking is no longer relevant. I am learning that past behaviour certainly does affect future outcomes, particularly in my relationship with my body and the planet. I am learning to understand that my thoughts and perception create my world. I am also learning that to be truly happy I need to be mindful of the present.

Our link to water and its connection to the divine and sacred is something that stretches back into the very mists of time 'for this blue planet' my home, your home; is a watery planet and it is from water that we owe our very existence. Water is a living consciousness that has been with us since the beginning of time. It flows through us connecting us to it and each other. I hope that in sharing this practice you feel that connection and I wish you all the wonder that is this practice, this way of living, whatever your personal journey. In working with the element of water we can dive deep within ourselves, exploring our depths and bringing up the pearls that lie within. May your journey be to the depths of your own being and may you find the treasures that lie within

Blessed be

Gratitudes

I am deeply grateful to Dion Fortune who wrote the book *The Sea Priestess*. Her inherent wisdom and ability to tell story is magical and I thank her for this gift.

Thank you to all of the wonderful women and men who call themselves Priestess and Priest and for all of the fantastic work you do and the friendship and love you bestow.

Thank you to my husband who is always there for me, taking care of me and walking through life with me as a true partner.

Thank you to my darling sons, who are brave and courageous in living their lives to the full and who live the dream.

Thank you to my mother for always being there to listen.

Thank you to my family who love me unconditionally.

Thank you Goddess for being there for me whatever is happening in my life, for loving me and holding me.

Thank you for this precious Earth this wonderful blue planet and all its creatures.

Bibliography

Baring, Anne and Jules Cashford, *The Myth of the Goddess, evolution of an image*, Arkana Books, Penguin 1993

Cooper, Diane, *2012 and Beyond*, Findhorn Press 2009

Dyer, Dr Wayne W, *Inspiration your Ultimate Calling*, Hay House 2006

Flem-Ath Rand and Colin Wilson, *The Atlantis Blue print*, Time Warner books 2000

Fortune, Dion, *The Sea Priestess*, Weiser Books 2003

Jones, Kathy, *Priestess of Avalon, Priestess of the Goddess*, Ariadne Publications 2006

Lilly, Sue and Simon, *Crystal, Colour and Chakra Healing*, Hermes House 2003, 2010

Matthews, Caitlin and John, *Ladies of the Lake*, Thorsons, 1992

Paulson, Genevieve Lewis, *Kundalini and the Chakras Evolution in this Lifetime a Practical Guide*, Llewellyn publications 2010

Villoldo, Alberto, *Courageous Dreaming, how Shamans Dream the World into Being* ,Hay House 2008

Weinstein, Marion, *Positive Magic*, New Page Books 2002

About the Author

Louise Tarrier lives in South Dorset, close to Poole harbour and the start of the Jurassic coastline. She has always lived close to the sea both in the UK and Australia, which she also call home and has a natural affinity with all things watery.

Her love of the Goddess and women's spirituality has been something that has anchored her life over many years. She walks the path of a Priestess. After having spent many years as an Accountant working for a large international business, she now runs her own holistic practice, where she specialises in women's health and spirituality, offering workshops and healing practices based on the teaching practices within the book.

For further information or to contact Louise visit her website at www.onedropof.co.uk